There is Hope

There is Hope

Sheryl Marie McDonald LMT.

ISBN: 978-1-4497-5222-4 (sc)

Scripture taken from the King James Version of the Bible.

WestBow Press books may be ordered through booksellers or by contacting:

WestBow Press
A Division of Thomas Nelson
1663 Liberty Drive
Bloomington, IN 47403
www.westbowpress.com
1-(866) 928-1240

Library of Congress Control Number: 2012908861

Printed in the United States of America

WestBow Press rev. date: 08/15/2012

In Loving Memory of Husband
Dr. Gene Joseph Cox
March 5, 1965- March 2, 2012

A life of struggle. A life of emptiness. A life of no purpose or meaning. That has been a life lived without the ingredient of hope. Hope is that one thing that keeps us looking forward. Forward to our future, with all of its possibilities. Believing that the best is yet to come. It keeps us looking ahead and not to our past with all of its regrets. And it also keeps us looking further beyond our immediate circumstances. For this too shall pass! Hope is that awesome power that motivates us to keep going when everything and everyone may be telling us to just give up!

A Powerful Hope!

You know we have a hope
that is steadfast and true.
One that we can count on
in every storm we go through.

A hope that we can
surely rest upon.
This powerful hope
is Jesus, God's Son.

He is the anchor
for my storm-tossed soul.
When the waves and billows
around me do roll.

He just says, "Peace"
and the waves be still.
Oh! He is a powerful hope!
I trust him to do his mighty will.

I can hold onto him,
to hold my ship together.
He is my anchor
in all kinds of weather.

Steadfast, unmovable, unshakeable,
I can count on him not to float away.
This anchor that I have,
doesn't rock, diminish or sway.

This anchor holds me
all the night and also all of my day.
For I can trust him to do
exactly what his word doth say.

So with Jesus as my anchor,
I can rest in hope.
Through this world's storms,
by his Word, I can cope!

Let's face it and get real! As long as we are out on this sea of life there will be storms. Jesus says in John 16:33, "These things I have spoken unto you, that in me ye might have peace. In the world ye shall have trouble; but be of good cheer; I have overcome the world." Jesus says that even though in this world we shall have trouble, but because of him we will have peace. We have peace knowing he holds us in the middle of those storms.

He Holds Me Through The Storm

Oh! Lord I praise you,
for your perfect peace
you give me everyday.
No matter what befalls me,
no matter what comes my way.

The sun may shine
or clouds may arise,
or skies may be bright blue.

But through good or bad,
I know Precious Savior,
I can always trust in you.

The winds may blow, the shadows fall,
the lightning may light up the sky.
But through all the storms, and amidst all the panic
my Father guards with his eye.

His mighty angels are always
watching over my soul.
And for this to him I am thankful,
though the billows may roll.

Just the knowledge he holds me,
it calms all of my fears.
It puts a smile on my face,
and washes away all of my tears.

There is no way I could live my life on this earth without the hope I have in Jesus. This world sometimes brings so much heartache that without Jesus I could never, ever bear it. I just do not know where I would go without being able to go to him with all of my cares.

I Thank You Lord For Hope

Thank you, Lord,
for your blessed Hope.
When troubles hit
and I no longer can cope.

I know somehow
you will turn trouble around
It won't last very long.
For Lord I know,
you use even trouble
to make me true and strong.

So I thank you Lord for hope
when things happen,
I just don't understand.
I have hope of sometime soon
being in a better land.

A land free from darkness,
crying, tears, heartache,
pain and despair.
Thank you Lord for Hope,
knowing you are going to come
and take me over there!

I have hope
no matter what,
this life here brings.
And just knowing you, Dear Lord,
are with me,
my heart truly sings.

You may be saying, "Well it is good you have hope, at least somebody does, because I don't." And you may be saying, "You don't know my situation. Things are just too bad for me." Well! There is nothing impossible with God!

There Is Always Hope!

I don't care
how bad it may seem.
I know a God,
who does redeem.

There is always hope,
for you and me.
Look up to Jesus,
he will change what you see.

The problem may not change,
in just one night.
Trust Jesus by faith,
and not by sight.

So there is never
a hopeless situation,
when we praise the God of all Hope,
every tongue, tribe and nation.

For with God all things are possible.
There is always Hope.
Nothing is so bad
that you cannot cope.

For Jesus is there
everywhere you go.
Oh! Don't you believe?
Oh! Don't you know?

He's promised to take care
of your every need.
So rejoice and look up,
my Lord doth intercede!

So many times Satan, (the enemy of our souls) tries to rob us of our hope, therefore stealing our purpose, meaning, joy, strength and peace. He doesn't realize he is not in control at all and that God is! God may allow him to do things to us, and God may allow him to think he is in control, but he is not. And no matter what Satan may try to do to destroy us, God will always turn it around for our good and for his glory. We can trust in the Lord to take care of us no matter what! He loves you so much. Hear him saying to you:

"Trust Me"

I know you are hurting,
and things are hard.
But trust me.
Not one thing in your life, will I discard.

Everything,
I am turning around for good.
Even though it doesn't happen
on the timing you think it should.

Even though the miracle you need
looks no where in sight.
Trust me,
everything will be alright.

Trust me, for I am Alpha and Omega,
the Beginning and the End.
Trust me, for I am
your very best friend.

Trust me when tempted
to worry and fret.
Rest in me, my child,
your needs will be met!

Don't try to always
figure things out.
Lean on me, it's going to be alright
without a doubt.

Trust me when things happen
you just don't understand.
Don't ever forget my child,
I am holding your hand.

And though I slay you, trust me.
As Job said in the days of old.
And the more you trust me,
watch as the blessings unfold.

For I am the same
yesterday, today and forever.
Though circumstances change
remember, I change never!

So rest patiently in my arms
and just enjoy being with me,
Rejoice in my love,
it is going to be alright, you will see!

You may say, "How can I rejoice? Things in my life are so out of control. And I'm used to being in control." Well, there comes a time to let go of control. Jesus comes to us down this highway of life, when we're exhausted, tired and so weary. We've had enough of our way. We've gone down every road and it seems we've met every dead end. Maybe it is time to give up and let Jesus take over!

On Our Journey

Sometimes when we first get saved
it is often like traveling in a car.
All excited for our journey to begin,
but as we travel, our goal seems so far.

We get tired and weary
and say we can't go another mile.
Then Jesus says, "Let me
take the wheel awhile.
Just rest your weary soul
and I'll help you
reach your goal."

He tells me not to look
at all the obstacles in our way.
Just trust in me and I'll get you
to where you are going someday.

I say it is too long and too hard
and I sometimes want to turn around.
But then I see how far he's brought me
then I know I'm Heaven Bound!

When we let Jesus take control of our lives and give him the steering wheel, we have love, peace, hope, joy and all of his goodness. And when we give Jesus total control and commit to him, we have everything we need. We no longer have to search endless long miles to find satisfaction for our souls. Nor do we have to cling to everything and everyone to fill up our empty souls. Jesus will see to it that we never run on empty.

Running on Empty

Running on empty
down this highway of life.
Bound and determined
no longer to live in strife.

I take a long look at
all the roads I have traveled.
Coming apart at the seams
and feeling a bit unraveled,

I begin to think
there has got to be a better way!
For this road I'm on,
I care no longer to stay.

I've tried every road
or so I have thought.
But all those roads have left me
empty, confused and distraught.

Then behind me I see a road
I somehow passed by.
How I overlooked it,
I can't imagine why.

For there were signs
leading and guiding all of the way.
Then the light shined
like the newness of day.

I missed it
because of my fear, doubt and dismay.
Oh! Lord, forgive me!
Help me travel on your road, I pray.

All the roads I went down
left me alone and suffering.
Because of a lot of junk,
I was left carrying.

And because of a lot of baggage
and a heavy, heavy load,
I overlooked and was blind
to God's heavenly road.

For on his road we have to keep
our eyes upon him.
For if we look at just our problems,
our sight will go dim.

We won't see clear
the road that we should take.
But our Lord will give us vision
so we won't go the wrong road by mistake.

Down his road he will fill us
with grace and mercy to make us smile.
He will fill us with love, joy and happiness,
enough to go every mile.

And no longer, "Running on Empty"
will you be.
Keep your eyes off of your problems, but on Jesus,
and his highway you will see!

When we are no longer running on empty, we won't be scared of running out of gas and being stranded. Have you ever wanted to go somewhere but you did not have enough gas in your car, nor money to go where you wanted? It probably left you feeling very frustrated and aggravated. You felt very limited to what you could do in life at that moment. There are people like that right now, spiritually speaking. They are frustrated, aggravated and feeling very limited in life. They are living in worry and fear of whether they are going to make it or not. God does not want us living like that! He wants us to live life to the fullest and enjoy the ride.

Enjoy the Ride!

Please, have your way, oh, Lord.
Though I have no idea what is coming my way.
Take over my life.Have your way, Oh, Lord.
That's all my heart can say.

For I have driven to this same dead end
over and over again.
Around and around this circle,
so many times I have been.

Help me get out of the driver's seat.
And let you have control.
Lord, drive me to the still waters
where you restore my soul.

Lord, help me never tell you what to do,
nor tell you how to drive.
For when I really

let go of the wheel then I am truly alive.

Have your way, oh, Lord,
Help me forget where I just left,drive me forward on.
Help me look straight ahead
and drive me to where I have never gone.

For Lord, if you don't take
ahold of this wheel and drive,
I will never make it to my home.
I will never arrive.

For only you, Lord, can drive me
through the darkness, and safely through the fog.
Only you, Lord, can drive me
around every hole and around every log.

For I can't see around the next bend,
or what is up ahead.
I can only make it home,
if by you, lord, I am led.

Lord, help me when I am riding along
and looking at the sights.
Help me not forget how far we've already made it,
through so many, many nights.

And, Lord, one thing I have learned
by my observation,
is to not panic, when it looks like
I am not going to make it, to my final destination.

For, Lord, you tell me ever so gently
to not be frightened.
For you, Lord, have the wheel, and knowing that
all of my burdens are truly lightened.

Help me to just be still
and Rejoice, Rejoice, Rejoice!
Knowing you are God
help me to praise you with all of my voice.

Just knowing, Lord Jesus,
you are driving me home and you are right by my side.
Knowing you have the wheel,
I am free to just praise you, and "Enjoy the Ride."

When you give Jesus control of your life, he will not wreck you! He will lead you safely home. He will never abandon you. He will never leave you nor forsake you. He will go before you and prepare the way. He knows where you are at this very second. He knows where you are going. So trust him to lead you safely home. Look to him and do not turn to the left or right, unless he tells you otherwise. Follow him every step. For he is the Way, the Truth, and the Life. Jesus will lead you safely home.

He Will Lead You Safely Home!

When I've exhausted
all of my plans,
dead ends I can't count
on both of my hands.

Sleepless nights out in the cold,
dark weather.
Not knowing what or who
was keeping me together.

Friends I thought I had
left me one by one.
Where are they now
When the day is done?

Where are they
when I can't find my way?
Oh, Lord, I'm so lonely,
to you, I pray!

You hear my desperate call.
Help me
lest I fall.

I can't make it without you
not another day.
Oh, Lord, help me
to find my way.

Then you tell me, Lord,
ever so sweetly, you will be my guide.
You will lead me, safely home
to the other side.

For you are the one who has made the way.
Down this road you know every bend.
You know every turn, bump and hole.
And you are already at its end.

Though I can only see
with my natural eyes just a few feet,
You, Lord, see the beginning and end
when one day we shall meet.

You know every hill, every valley,
every mountain, that I will have to cross.
You know every blessing,
every gain given and also every loss.

Knowing you've gone before me
preparing the way that I should take.
I can trust you will lead me safely home,
Me, never ever to forsake.

Jesus knows every single thing about your life. He has a plan all mapped out especially for you. He has a blueprint with your name on it. Oh! If people could really get ahold of that fact there would be less violence, boredom and loneliness. We would be living a life filled with purpose like God intends.

He Has A Plan For Your Life!

Don't just sit there
in doubt and despair.
Look up to Jesus,
and on him cast all of your care.

For he has such a wonderful plan
designed just for you.
He loves you oh, so much.
and he watches everything you do.

So get rid of feeling all blue,
discouraged and down.
Jesus loves you,
talk to him for he is always around.

I call thee by name, God is telling you that now. Before he formed you in the womb he knew you. He knew your name. God has your life all planned. Before you were born, God knew you. Just as he told the Prophet of old, (Jeremiah), "Before I formed you in the belly I knew thee." He knew you! You are not a mistake! You are here for a reason!

You Have a Purpose

You have a purpose,
you have a goal.
No more sitting idle,
you have to go.

You got to tell this world
while there is time to tell.
Jesus saved you
from Hell.

You have to tell them
while you can.
Share his love
all over this land.

Tell the gospel story
how he set you free.
Tell them he is alive,
and he loves you and me!

So if you are sitting and wondering
what you are doing down here.
God has a purpose.
Ask him and he will make it clear.

Ask him to reveal
his perfect plan for you.
For he has a special task
especially through you, for him to do.

There is a work.
There is a will.
There is a calling,
for you to fulfill.

There is a purpose.
There is a plan.
There is a reason,
that you are here in this land.

For you have come into the kingdom,
for such a time as this.
Seek the Lord's will, and you will have
peace, happiness, joy and bliss.

When we finally get ahold of the fact that God put us here, and we are here for a reason, we can get up in the morning realizing every day is a gift. We don't have to wake up and live in dread and waste our days. We can wake up and welcome each new day with anticipation.

Anticipation

Help me, Heavenly Father,
have anticipation toward my future.
Help me see with you,
it is a wonderful, exciting adventure.

I wake up never knowing
what the day will bring.
But I know you are ever with me,
knowing that only, my heart can sing.

And no matter what
this life brings from year to year.
Help me walk with you,
and not succumb to fear.

Let me remember you are guiding my footsteps.

You are holding my hand.
You know where I am going,
and you do (for me also) have a marvelous plan.

Things may not happen
the way I see fit.
When they don't, please help me
not to throw my hands up and quit.

Help me rise above
each problem that comes my way.
Help me not focus on my self
or on the pain, come what may.

Help me focus only on you, Lord
whether the way is dark or plain.
Help me worship you every day,
the rest of my days that remain.

Help me live with anticipation
on how you are going to bring me through.
And help me, Heavenly Father
to totally rely on you!

It is all a matter of how we see things. If we keep our eyes on Jesus we can learn from our struggles, and not get bitter. We can give them to our Lord, and he will help us see things as he sees them. No matter what we are going through. So many times when going through troubles, trials, sorrow, heartache or pain, it could be so easy to get overwhelmed and just focus on all the bad. We need to take a lesson from Paul. He was a man who went through some suffering. It was not always smooth sailing for him. Three times he was shipwrecked. Five times he received thirty-nine stripes from the Jews. He was stoned. He went through perils (dangers), in waters, perils from his own countrymen, perils by the heathen, perils in the sea, and perils among false brethren. He had nights of sleeplessness, weariness and painfulness. Nights of hunger and thirst in cold and nakedness. He also had a responsibility of taking care of churches. How did he keep from getting overwhelmed with all he experienced? He learned to glory in those things that kept him dependent on God's strength. He focused on God and not on the circumstances. After all the things Paul suffered, he was still able to rejoice. Paul says in Philippians 4:4: "Rejoice in the Lord always; and again I say, Rejoice. Let your self-control be known unto all men. The Lord is at hand. v. 6 Be careful for nothing; but in everything by prayer and supplication with thanksgiving let your requests be made known unto God. v. 7 And the peace of God, which passeth all understanding shall keep your hearts and minds through Christ Jesus." v. 8 Paul also says, "Finally, brethren, whatsoever things are true, whatsoever things are honest, whatsoever things are just. Whatsoever things are pure, whatsoever things are lovely, whatsoever things are of good report; if there be any virtue, and if there be any praise, think on these things, v. 9 Those things, which ye have both learned, and received and heard, and seen in me, do. And the God of peace shall be with you."

When going through a difficult time we need to do what Paul says to do. Don't just think about how bad your situation is. Think on things that are true. He is true to his Word. Think on those things that are of good report. Don't believe the report the doctor is telling you. Don't believe the report your bank statement says. Believe God's report. His report says we are healed. Satan wants you to keep your eyes on the bad things of life. Whether it is a painful past, a terrible present, or an unseen future. Or maybe you can't stop thinking about what someone has done to you. Or your bills may look like they are piling up. Satan knows if he can keep you miserable over your problems, it will weigh you down. And he knows he is in trouble if you let go of those burdens, past, present and future ones and give them to Jesus, and start thinking of Jesus and what his word says. God promises in Isaiah, "Thou wilt keep him in perfect peace whose mind is stayed on thee." I am not saying that everything is going to turn out exactly the way we want it. But I know a God who turns all things around for our good and his glory. No matter what Satan throws at us, it cannot harm a child of God! It may hurt us and break our hearts, but it cannot harm us because Jesus knows how to use every situation that we go through. What Satan thinks will destroy us, God will use it as an opportunity to reveal his awesome power in our lives. He will use every opportunity to transform us into the image of Jesus.

Yes, he will use every trial, every pain to transform us into his image. That is what we all need! To be transformed into the image of God's Son, our Savior, Lord Jesus Christ. For example, every time someone says something very hurtful to us and we feel like telling them off. We need to remind ourselves of what Jesus would do. See, Satan will do everything he can to cause us to stop worshipping God. How many of us when having a very difficult day, have taken our frustrations out on someone else? Most of the time those we are closest to. Too many times we do that with God. We get disappointed when things have not turned out the way we have expected them to and sometimes we take it out on Jesus. You may say, "I don't do that, I love Jesus, I don't take my problems out on him." Sometimes our actions speak louder than words. When we start grumbling and complaining and stop worshipping and praising our Lord, Satan has us right where he wants us. Right along with a host of countless others who have fallen victim to his subtle attacks. We need to not forget his tricks to get us to get our eyes off of Jesus and the wonderful things he says in his Word, onto the negative aspects of our life. It is no new trick with Satan to get us to focus on anything other than what God tells us. He has been doing that since the beginning of creation. Let's not fall for his tricks any longer. Let's reflect on what God tells us. Let's reflect more on wonderful, positive things. Let's not dwell on negative things that only birth discouragement, defeat and bitterness. Even when thinking over our past, instead of reflecting on all of the bad circumstances that have occurred, let's reflect more on the good ones. Even though God does use those bad circumstances for his glory, let's still focus more on the good ones.

Reflect On The Good

Oh, Lord, Help me to reflect more
on the good things of my life.
Help me to forget
all of the pain and all of the strife.

Let me remember times in my life
when the sun has shone.
Help me see all the good things
that I have were from you and you alone.

Sometimes the pain in my life
has blinded me from the good.
Thank you, Lord, for opening my eyes
and helping me see as I should.

For you didn't want me
to stop at the pain.
You wanted me to look beyond.
You'd tell me, come on, I have Heaven to gain.

So keep going you kept telling me
and look to eternity, forgetting the past.
For this world and its problems
are not going to last.

Lord, you'd tell me great peace I have,
so in nothing be offended.
Vengeance was yours, to trust you,
me, you always defended.

So, Lord, whenever I start letting
the bad get me down,
thank you for keeping a smile on my face,
and for taking away my frown.

For only you, Lord Jesus, can help me
gain a new perspective.
Only when I reflect on you,
and good things, that is when I truly live!

Sometimes the hurt we feel may be so intense and our circumstances may be just unbelievably bad, that we just cannot get beyond them. We see only what it is doing to us in the natural. But if we stop and look up to Jesus and get our eyes off of our problems, Jesus will give you a new perspective. He will shed light on your situation. He will light up your life. He will show you what is really going on. What we see and feel may not necessarily be true. The only truth is Jesus and what his Word says. Even if we are going through some kind of problem from our own making, he will forgive you and give you direction and help. Maybe we blew up at someone and said some things we shouldn't have said. Or maybe someone has done or said something to hurt you. Whatever it is, just give it to Jesus, and somehow he will turn it around and use it for the gospel's sake.

Furtherance of the Gospel

I've been through many trials
while living here below.
I understand now
they were only to help me grow.

For how else would I know
how much God takes care of me?
For in every heartache
he always sets me free.

Everything Satan thought
to destroy me it should,
My God has always
turned it around for my good.

He takes my pain and sorrow.
And all of my trouble and heartache.
Even my failures and weaknesses,
and uses for the Gospel's sake.

I never need to question why
this trial has happened to me.
I ask him what he wants me to learn
and to open my eyes and see.

We have to realize we will have trials. We will have times of persecution, times of not knowing what is going on. And we may question why is this happening to me? That is when we need to take a look at Joseph. Joseph was born a long time ago. He was a normal person like us. He was born in a different time than us, (we are all born in the timing God has planned). The point is he was just like us. Well, he had a dream that all of his brothers were one day going to bow down to him. He confronted them about the dream and they did not like it. Joseph had eleven brothers and a sister. Joseph was bold in telling his Dad and all of his brothers about the dream God gave him. Because he was the second to the last out of all of his Dad's children. His Dad (Jacob) had thirteen children. I can just see this little pee-wee standing up to all of his family and telling them it's okay, you just wait one day you are all going to bow down to me, God showed me. I can see him now trying to convince them what God had showed him. Don't expect anyone to be as excited as you are because you may be very disappointed. Not everyone will see the vision like you have. Not even your own relatives. Not unless they are a part in that vision. In fact, you may tell someone what God has showed you and they may turn on you and hate you and be very jealous of you. They may even want to kill you. Like Joseph's brothers, who were very offended with him and they said, you're crazy, we're not bowing down to you! No way! No how! Then they threw him in a pit. What happened was Joseph's brothers were out in She'chem feeding the flocks and Jacob called for Joseph and told him to go see how his brothers were doing. Well, Joseph did as his father told him to and he did not find his brothers in She'chem, but he found them in Dothan, because they went from She'chem to Dothan. His brothers saw him coming afar off, they conspired against him to slay him. In Genesis 37:20, they said, "Come now therefore, and let us slay him, and cast him into some pit, and we will say some evil beast hath devoured him; and we shall see what will become of his dreams." You can read the rest of the story of Joseph in Genesis because it doesn't end there, they did not kill him but threw him in a pit. Reuben (Joseph's older brother) talked his other brothers into just throwing him into a pit. Then while they were eating a company of Ish'-me-el-lites came by and his brothers decided instead of leaving him in that pit to die, why not sell him and make a profit off of him, after all they had to do something with him. Now Reuben did not know that the other brothers had sold him. He returned to the pit and saw him gone he thought an animal got him or something. They all thought it was over for Joseph. Well, that dream Joseph had wasn't going to come true now was it? Or so they thought. When God gives a dream it will happen! Rest assured it will come to pass! But also be aware that Satan will try to kill that dream. He hates us and he is out to steal, kill and destroy us. But he can only go so far. God will allow him to go so far and then he will say, that's enough!

That's Enough!

While struggling along
with earthly care,
you may feel hurt and alone,
Without a true friend anywhere.

Others may mock, reject
and push you aside.
But just remember Jesus loves you
whatever betide.

There is nothing, no nothing
anyone can hide from our Heavenly Father's eyes.
So when others throw you in a lonely pit,
there is a God who hears your cries.

He sees when others are cruel
and they make you feel like a fool.
When you love our Lord
and try to go by the golden rule.

You may feel you can't go on
for the way is so rough.
Call on Jesus, and before long,
he'll come and say, "That's enough!"

I can remember when I was about twelve years old. My Mother drove a school bus when I was growing up, and sometimes we would stop at a little store called "Terry's." This particular day she stopped aside the road and handed me a list for me to go into the store and get what she needed. I stepped down from the steps and started to walk real fast. Well, all of a sudden, this big, ferocious dog came growling and running toward me. And it did not like me being on his territory. And I am telling you, he had no intentions of letting me into that store to get what I had to get. And frankly when I saw him I didn't think I would ever again need what was in that store in the first place. I thought I had already eaten my last meal that morning anyway. Well, I kept running farther away from the front of the store. And the whole time I was thinking this dog is going to get me for sure. He just kept coming at me and coming at me. Just when I thought it was all over for me, all of a sudden that dog stopped and then his head jerked back. Neither the dog nor I noticed the long chain that he was tied to. One end around his head and the other end to the fence behind the store. That dog was too angry to remember he had a chain around his neck that only went so far. That dog was out to kill me that day. I was too scared to notice the chain, all I could hear was his growling.And it all happened so fast but he could only go so far. I Corinthians 10:13 says, "There hath no temptation taken you but such as is common to man: But God is faithful, who will not suffer you to be tempted above that ye are able; but will with the temptation also make a way to escape, that ye may be able to bear it." I have sometimes read that and thought, Lord God you must think I can bear an awful lot, because you sure have brought me through a lot of heartaches. Have you ever said that? I have many times. Then I later found out that it had nothing to do with my strength, but in God's faithfulness, in making a way for me to escape so I would be able to bear my troubles. Had it not been simply for the fact that Jesus stepped in right in the nick of time, I would have perished. It is so good to know he has Satan on a leash. God will allow him to go just so far. And he will say that is enough!

We have to get it deep in our hearts that God is in control! There was a time in King David's life where he was being cursed by a wicked man named Shim'-me-i. In 2 Samuel 16:6-13 he says, "And he cast stones at David, and at all the servants of King David: and all the people and all the mighty men were on his right hand and on his left. 7. And thus said Shim-me-i when he cursed, Come out, come out, thou bloody man, and thou man of Be-li-al:" Then in verse 9 A-bi'-shai wanted to go and take off his head. And David tells him in verse 10, "What have I to do with you, ye sons of Ze-ru'-iah? So let him curse, because the Lord hath said unto him, Curse David. Who shall then say, Wherefore hast thou done so? 11. And David said to A-bi'-shai, and to all his servants. Behold, my son, which came forth of my own body, seeketh my life; how much more now may this Benjaminite do it? Let him alone, and let him curse; for the Lord hath bidden him. 12. It may be that the Lord will look on mine affliction, and that the Lord will repay me good for his cursing this day. 13. And as David and his men went by the way, Shim-e-i went along on the hillside over against him, and cursed as he went, and threw stones at him, and kicked up dust. 14. And the King, and all the people that were with him, came weary, and refreshed themselves there."

David knew his God was in control! Even when someone was cursing him. You may be in a situation like King David was in, where it seems that everyone around you is persecuting, cursing and calling you names. Someone or maybe a multitude may be falsely accusing you, as in King David's situation. You need to get it deep in your heart that not everyone is going to love you. Not everyone is going to care that you are a child of God. In fact, because you are a child of God, Jesus says in Matthew 10:22, "And ye shall be hated of all men for my name's sake: but he that endureth to the end shall be saved." And also in John 15:18-20, "If the world hate you, ye know that it hated me before it hated you. If ye were of the world, the world would love his own but because ye are not of the world, but I have chosen you out of the world, therefore the world hateth you. Remember the word that I said unto you, The servant is not greater than his lord. If they have persecuted me, they will also persecute you;' if they have kept my saying, they will keep yours also." Jesus warns us right there that we will be hated of all men, and if they have persecuted him, we will be persecuted also. We are not greater than him. David was persecuted and he was a king. John says in Revelation chapter one verse six, "And hath made us kings and priests unto God and his Father; to him be glory and dominion for ever and ever, A-men." Jesus was persecuted because he was Jesus. Because he was God. David was persecuted because he was King. We are persecuted because we are kings and priests. We need not grumble and complain when we are being cursed at, we need to rejoice because of the blessing coming our way because of others cursing us. As King David realized the blessing in knowing God. David realized that God was in control of everything, and if someone was cursing him, he knew God willed it. He didn't seek revenge and take matters into his own hands. But he let him curse, and he didn't try to stop him, by defending himself. He said to the servant that wanted to take off his head, let him alone. The Lord will reward me this day blessing for his cursing. He said, "The Lord will judge righteously concerning him and the man that was cursing him." In 1 Peter 2:20-23, "For what glory is it, if, when ye be buffeted for your faults ye shall take it patiently? But if, when ye do well, and suffer for it, ye take it patiently, this is acceptable with God. For even hereunto were ye called: because Christ also suffered for us, leaving us an example, that ye should follow his steps; Who did not sin, neither was guile found in his mouth; Who when he reviled,

reviled not again; when he suffered he threatened not; but committed himself to him that judgeth righteously."

I cannot tell you the messes I have made in my life, because I did not take this word to heart. Oh, I've read this many times, but during times of persecution, I would forget it. That is because too many times I would allow my heart to get hardened toward the people that were persecuting me. That was because most of the time it was my own family members that were mocking and criticizing me. I couldn't figure out why it was happening, they should love me, I thought. But God is teaching me, that everything is under his control, even if someone is coming against us. He will judge righteously. He sees everything! Proverbs 15:3 says, "The eyes of the Lord are in every place, beholding the evil and the good." We need not run from evil. If we have Jesus in our hearts he is greater than anything Satan throws at us. We need not isolate ourselves and slip into depression, discouragement and defeat. "Greater is he that is in us than he that is in the world."

There was a man named, "Elijah," who God used mightily upon this earth. Elijah was a great prophet of God. But there was a time in his life he allowed Satan to cause him to fear and it led to discouragement and depression. He even wanted to die. He just witnessed the greatest or one of the greatest victories in his life, yet he let one wicked woman named, "Jezebel" cause him to isolate himself in a cave. He heard that she was coming to kill him so he ran for his life. Instead of him standing in the power of God and telling her to bring it on, that God would deal with her, he ran the other way. I am not condemning Elijah, for I, like him, have done that many, many times. Too many that I do not care to mention. Even recently I went through a similar situation, like Elijah I felt like everyone was against me, and I was going through a very difficult time, and all I wanted to do was stay in my house and not talk to anyone, ever again. I was discouraged, disappointed and hurt over my circumstances, because things seemed like they were getting worse and here I was waiting on God to make them better. I couldn't figure out why. I was doing everything I thought I was supposed to do. I even got mad at God, because I thought he could change things if he wanted to, but instead he was letting me suffer. Why? Didn't he love me I'd ask? Elijah felt the same way, he slipped into self-pity, much like we sometimes can do. But God doesn't want us there, he wants us to move on. He wants us to overcome! He wants us to rise above all discouragement and defeat. He has given us the power to do so. You can read about Elijah in 1 Kings Chapter 17 – 2 Kings Chapter 2. In the story we read earlier about King David, he had hope that God would look at his situation and because he would let the Lord deal with his enemies, he did not retaliate. David kept his hope. Your hope is one of many things that Satan comes to take from you. You have to hold onto it and not let him have it. He will use others, sometimes even those that are close to us. In that story about David he could have let the curses of "Shim-e-i" destroy him. He could have cursed him back. He could have ran and got in self-pity, and blamed God. He could have whined to God, why are you letting him curse me like that God, I'm a sweet person why are you letting me go through this? He could have isolated himself and said, "That's it God, I have had it with wicked people, I am going home and I am never, ever speaking to anyone again! I am through with dealing with difficult people!" Or he even could have murdered that man that was cursing him. No, David did not do any of those things. Instead he gave it to God and waited on God to defend him. And he did not let that man get him bitter. He stayed in that place and God blessed him and used him there. That place that was used by the enemy to curse him, was also the place God chose to bless him and to use him as a blessing to others. In 2 Samuel 16:13 it says, "And as David and his men went by the way, Shim-e-i went along on the hillside over against him, and cursed as he went, and threw stones at him, and kicked up dust. And the King and all the people that were with him, came weary, and refreshed themselves there." Too many times in my own life I would let what one person had said to me affect how I would treat others, including my Lord Jesus Christ. I would allow what one negative person would say to me to affect me so bad, that I would think because they thought negatively of me, God and everyone else must also. I am learning now when one doesn't receive me to move on. By God's grace we can't let Satan, (the enemy of our souls) to steal our hope and joy, and to rob us of God's promise to bless us. In Matthew 10, Jesus sends his disciples out two by two, and tells them to go and preach the gospel, to heal the sick, cleanse the lepers, raise the dead, and cast out devils. Jesus says in verse 14, "And whosoever shall not receive you, nor hear your words, when ye depart out of that house or city, shake the dust off your feet. We have to just shake off what the devil throws at us. It may be people mocking us and criticizing us. It may be worries and concerns over our finances. Whatever is causing us to worry and fret we have a way out. In 1 Peter 5:7 he says, "Cast your cares upon the Lord for he careth for you Be sober, be vigilant; because your adversary, the devil as a roaring lion, walketh about, seeking whom he may devour; whom resist steadfast in the faith, knowing that the same afflictions are accomplished in your brethren that are in the world." It does not matter what you are going through right now, and it may seem the devil is coming at you with everything he has in him. He may be threatening or accusing you, but all is not hopeless. You can cast all of your cares on Jesus. Submit to Lord Jesus and resist the devil and he will flee from you. Getting back to that story about the dog, had I been nice to that dog, he would have torn me to shreds. It was pretty obvious he was not my friend. Too many times we treat Satan like he is our friend. We may not intentionally do that, but we do not resist him like we should. We too easily let him steal our hope, peace, love, joy and whatever else good we have. He will take everything if we let him. We have to remember he hates us and he is out to steal, kill and destroy us. When we resist him and submit to God it does not matter what happens to us we have hope. God will let Satan go only so far, and whatever happens to us, we can know we will be okay. With God, we can know everything will be all right. God may allow Satan to throw us in a pit. And just like Joseph, it may be right after God has given us a dream or vision about something awesome happening in our life. Something may happen to us totally opposite of the dream he has shone us. But just like Joseph hold onto your dream. Joseph held on to his dream that made him hope. He would not let the enemy of his soul get his hope. When he was shut up in a cold, dark dungeon, what kept him hanging on? Hope! The hope he had in his heart kept him from despair, bitterness, resentment and unforgiveness toward his brothers or towards God. He knew God was faithful no matter what had happened in his past and no matter what he was going through at that time. He knew it was somehow going to change! He knew his God doesn't change. And that same God that gave him that vision in his past, about his future, was the same God that was with him in that cold prison. Though the seasons (so to speak) had changed in his life, God's love never changed! It was still with him forever! So just like Joseph you may be going through what seems like spiritually the coldest, bleakest winter of your life. Don't get angry and bitter, for that will only change your circumstances for the worst. And especially don't get angry at God. He is the one that really loves you. No matter what season of life you are in spiritually, remember Jesus never changes, keep him always in your sight!

In The Seasons Of Your Life

No matter the season that you happen to be in,
there is one truth that yet remains.
That Jesus loves you through the winter
with all of its pains.

Through the Spring,
with all of its showers and rains.
Through the Summer with all of the heat.
Through the Fall, his love stays the same.

So in our lives there are different seasons,
that we all go through.
It is a fact, seasons change
for me and you.

There is one truth
that we can rest upon.
That God's love never changes,
and knowing just that, it keeps us hanging on.

It doesn't matter if you're in the Summer,

Spring, Winter or Fall.
Jesus will be with you,
he will be your all in all!

He will be with you
in every season of your life.
in the bitter Winter,
with winds of persecution, or cold winds of strife.

Or you may be in the Summer
in the warm sunshine, with the hot suns' rays.
Whatever the season,
keep Jesus with you all of your days.

You may be in the Fall,
when everything is changing.
No matter the season, Jesus loves you,
let him do a little rearranging.

Or you may be in the Spring of your life,
when everything seems rosy, everything just right.
Just remember whatever the seasons
Jesus never changes, keep him always in your sight.

When you know beyond a shadow of a doubt you know Jesus, you have nothing at all to fear. For you can run to him always and tell him everything on your mind continually. Oh, what an awesome thought! Oh, what an awesome blessing that we are not down here to fend for ourselves. We can go to Jesus anytime! Especially when we need help.

Lord, Help!

Lord, I come to you again,
with trouble on my mind.
I'm feeling so confused,

so helpless, so weary, so blind.

I don't understand,
for I know you led me here.
I've sought you and obeyed you,
and I know I've heard you clear.

I'm struggling with my doubts,
and I'm trying hard not to fear.
For I know Lord you are with me,
you are faithful to be near.

So what is going on?
I just don't understand.
I'm here in this wilderness,
and I want to be in my Promised Land.

I really thought things would be different,
than what they are right now.
But, Lord, even though I have these feelings,
I know in my heart you will bring me through somehow.

For you've been faithful so far to keep me,
you never, ever fail.
I know, Lord, with you no matter what,
I shall prevail!

So, Lord, even though
I don't know what is going on.
I trust in you, knowing that
with you the victory is already won!

When we trust someone, it does not mean we always have to see that one to trust them. It is easy to trust someone when that one is right there with us, every minute of the day. But do we trust that one when they are gone? Do we believe that one (maybe your husband or wife) is where they say they are going to be? Or doing what they are supposed to be doing? That is where real trust comes in. Sometimes in our relationship with our Lord, we may not always see or understand what he is doing, and sometimes we definitely can't figure him out. That is where real trust comes in. For there are times when our Lord is at work, and we may not see him, but he has given us his word. And even though he says he would never leave us nor forsake us, there are times when walking with him, that he will go on before us, and work his perfect will. And during those times Satan may come and tell us that our Lord has left us and he may tempt us to just give up. But again that is where real trust comes in. When all of Hell is coming against us, trying to steal our hope, with his weapons of discouragement, resentment and strife, that is the time to trust our Lord. Though you can't see him, trust him that he is working and he is doing what he says he will do. Trust means: credence, confidence, dependence, reliance, and faith. Even though we can't see God with our natural eyes, he is there!

"God is There"

So many times I've cried out,
to God in deep despair.
I sometimes even wondered
if he was really there.

I said impatiently, "How long
does this pain have to go on?"
Jesus then reminds me,
when I am weak, he is strong.

Though the storms are raging
high around you,
just trust in me
for I feel the things you do.

Every hurt you've had.

Every tear you've shed.
It was for you too,
that I died and bled.

But I arose the third day
and am no longer dead.
And he says, "My child, I know
the very number of hairs on your head.

Please don't doubt,
but only believe,
and all of the things I've promised,
you will receive.!"

Trust the Lord, he is there. 1 Peter 1:6 says, "Wherein ye greatly rejoice though now for a season, if need be, ye are in heaviness through manifold temptations; that the trial of your faith, being much more precious than of gold that perisheth, though it be tried with fire, might be found unto praise and honor and glory at the appearing of Jesus Christ. Whom having not seen, ye love, in whom, though now ye see him not, yet believing, ye rejoice with joy unspeakable, and full of glory: Receiving the end of your faith, even the salvation of your souls." Sometimes we have a tendency to believe the Lord is with us if we are experiencing his blessings, or his miracles. And then when we go through trials, we tend to think he has left us, or we have somehow stepped out of his will. Sometimes even right in the middle of his will we will go through trials or storms. None of us like to hear that, But God did not promise us that there would be no trials if we followed him. He did promise us that he would be with us. Sometimes it is hard to keep our hope when it seems like our life is falling apart. It is then that we cannot forget the faithfulness of Jesus. It is then that we have to keep our eyes and faith in Jesus. He has promised never to leave us nor forsake us. The disciples experienced a time they went through a horrifying storm. In Luke 8:22-25 Jesus and his disciples got into a ship, and he told them they were all going over to the other side. It did not matter if a storm came up along the way. Jesus said they were going over to the other side. How many of us do that? We get out on the sea of life with Jesus, all gung ho and ready to go. Then circumstances change beyond our control. A storm comes, the wind begins to blow, the water begins to rise and it appears we are going under and going under quickly. How many times do we scream out to Jesus in sheer terror thinking he has brought us this far and now he is going to let us drown? When circumstances change, don't fear! God may use it as an opportunity to show his awesome power. So welcome change, and let God use it.

"Welcome Change"

Change is a word
not many people want to hear.
Change to some brings
nothing but torment, worry and fear.

But we must look at change not as a foe,
but as a faithful friend.
For when change comes in our life it does not mean,
your life is over, that it is the end.

Change comes not to harm us,
but only to do us good.
When we trust in the Lord,
and wait on him as we should.

Even though it seems that God
is coming much too late.
Good things will come to those,
who hope in the Lord and patiently wait.

So don't panic when change
suddenly enters and alters your plan.
Welcome it and rejoice,

and accept it as a friend to man.

Never forget God knows where you are going
and everything is going to all work out.
Even through change keep your faith in him,
believe in him and never doubt.

God knows where you are at.
When change comes and closes one door,
it is no need to fear,
for our Lord Jesus has gone on before.

Jesus will open
another door just up ahead.
So there is no reason to live
each day in fear and dread.

And just knowing Jesus is with us
that is reason enough to rejoice.
So no matter the changes I'm still
going to praise him with my voice.

For he is the same yesterday, today and forever.
And that truth I can rest upon.
So when change comes, I'll hold onto Jesus,
and his strong arms I'll lean on.

When change comes does Jesus have to ask us like he did those disciples, "Where is your faith?" When going through storms or trials don't look at the circumstances that surround you. Look up to Jesus and he will lift you up. He will not let you go under. He will not let you drown in this sea of life.

"Sea of Life"

When in the sea of despair,
grasping, drowning from care.
Jesus reaches down and whispers,
"He is there."

Oh, He'll not let you perish
if you put your faith in him.
Trust him to hold you and deliver
out of your sea of sin.

Believe his word,
for it is your lifeline for your soul.
You can grab onto it,
It's an anchor for you to hold.

Don't ever let it go.
For it will take you safely to the shore.
It will bring you out of darkness,
and light your way forevermore.

So in this sea of life
and the waves around me roll.
Jesus whispers, "Do not fear,"
sweetly to my soul.

He'll say you've called on me,
I'll not fail you, my dear.
You'll not perish
for I am here!

Just look up
and don't look down
at the pressures
that surround.

Keep your eyes
and faith in me.
And my Glory
you will see!

For I'll not let you go under
in this sea of strife.
For if you believe in me
you have everlasting life!

When we know Jesus it does not mean that we will never experience storms. Because in this world we will experience all kinds of situations. We experience valleys, storms, mountains, wildernesses, plains, hills, cliffs, and also beautiful sunrises. All of these we go through on our journey while we are here below. Some of these circumstances give us pleasure, ecstasy, peace and joy beyond our highest expectations. However, some of these circumstances are not so wonderful. They leave us confused, heartbroken, terrified, disappointed, and discouraged. Even though we may experience all these kinds of emotions, we can choose to not let these negative feelings overtake us. John says in 1 John 5:4, "For whatsoever is born of God overcometh the world; and this is the victory that overcometh the world, even our faith." And Paul says in Galatians 2:20, "I am crucified with Christ; nevertheless I live; yet not I, but Christ liveth in me; and the life which I now live in the flesh I live by the faith of the Son of God, who loved me, and gave himself for me." It does not matter what we go through, we can allow Jesus Christ to live in us and through us. Then we can rise up above our circumstances. Isaiah says in Isaiah 43:1,2 "But now thus saith the Lord, that created thee, O Jacob, and he that formed thee, O Israel, Fear not: For I have redeemed thee, I have called thee by thy name; thou art mine. 2. When thou passest through the waters, I will be with thee; and through the rivers, they shall not overflow thee; when thou walkest through the fire, thou shalt not be burned; neither shall the flame kindle upon thee."

"Jesus Holds My Head Above the Waters"

Old Satan you thought you had me.
you thought that trial would do me in.
But I have news for you, Old Satan,
my God has delivered me once again!

You thought I was going under,
for the last and final time,
but Jesus held me above the waters
And now I am doing just fine.

so you see Old Satan, no matter how high the waters,
and no matter how deep the flood,
I shall be all right, I shall be fine,
for you can never wash away the blood!

No matter what the enemy does, he cannot take the blood of Jesus from your soul. You may walk through the fire, but you will not be burned. Oh, You may go through the rivers, but they will not overflow you! And God promises, when you pass through the waters he will be with you. There is nothing that a child of God goes through that can harm them. Satan may hate you and seek to destroy you, but he cannot when you are covered in the blood! When you have asked Jesus to forgive you of your sins and wash you clean in his blood, he does just that!

"Only the Blood of Jesus"

You can have your mansions
and your silver and gold.
Don't care to have just that,
when my life story is told.

For that is not going to save me,
when for me the death angel comes.
That's not going to change his tune.
When to me death songs he hums.

For only the blood of Jesus
Will tell my plight.
Only the blood of Jesus,
will decide darkness from light.

Only the blood of Jesus,
will decide my fate.
Only the blood of Jesus,
will get me inside of Heaven's Gate.

Years ago God's chosen people, the Israelites, were in bondage to the Egyptians. The Egyptians made them serve with hard bondage for forty, long, hard years. God raised up a deliverer named Moses. God knew Moses was on the backside of the desert tending sheep. As he had planned, It was Time . . . Time for Deliverance! God calls to Moses from a burning bush, and Moses turns aside and answers. God instructs Moses to go to Egypt and command Pharaoh to let God's people go. Pharaoh out of the hardness of his heart made the Israelites work harder than ever before. He was not about to let them go. He needed them to work for him. Pharaoh said to Moses and Aaron, "Who is the Lord, that I should obey his voice to let Israel go? I know not the Lord, neither will I let Israel go." Pharaoh was King of Egypt, and may have had everything he wanted, or so he thought, but there was one thing that was lacking for sure in Pharaoh's heart and life. What was it? Faith! Faith is belief in the value, or trustworthiness in what Moses was telling him. He did not want to listen to Moses at all, after all he thought he was in charge. Jesus says in Matthew 10:40, 41 "He that receiveth you receiveth me, and he that receiveth me, receiveth him that sent me. He that receiveth a Prophet in the name of a prophet shall receive a prophet's reward: and he that receiveth a righteous man in the name of a righteous man shall receive a righteous man's reward." Pharaoh did not receive a prophet's reward because he would not listen. Instead his hardness of heart cost himself and all of Egypt to suffer. We have to realize that what we do does matter. It will affect others along the way, whether good or bad.

"Someday Along the Way"

Someday along the way
it will touch some soul.
It will bring the lost to Jesus
and make them whole.

What we do it will matter
whether good or bad.
To make others
happy or sad.

Don't forget we're sowing seeds
as we walk from day to day.
Don't forget they will touch,
Some soul along the way.

There will be someone behind us.
Someone following you.
So remember it does matter.
Whatever you do.

You may say,
you're not hurting anyone.

But you are if you're not leading them
to Jesus God's Son.

What we do it does count,
for all of Eternity.
So live your life for Jesus,
so him others will see.

That little dime that you gave
that didn't seem like much.
Someday along the way
a precious heart it will touch.

Someday along the way
it will touch some soul.
It will bring the lost to Jesus,
and make them whole.

What we do it will matter,
whether good or bad.
To make others
happy or sad.

We all want love, happiness, peace, joy and hope. We would be lying if we said we didn't care. Sometimes when we feel like we aren't getting the love we need, we may act like we don't care. But deep down we all want those things. We need to realize maybe we need to give first what we are wanting. If we reap what we sow, maybe we need to sow love, joy, kindness, respect, friendship, or mercy and expect those things to come back. Because what we sow, we shall reap. In Galatians 6:7, God's word tells us, "Be not deceived; God is not mocked: for whatsoever a man soweth, that shall he also reap. 8. For he that soweth to his flesh shall of the flesh reap death; but he that soweth to the Spirit shall of the Spirit reap life everlasting. 9. And let us not be weary in well-doing; for in due season we shall reap, if we faint not." Getting back to the story of Pharaoh, he chose to sow to his flesh, and he reaped death. Spiritual death and also physical death. It cost him the death of his firstborn. That does not mean if you have experienced a death, that you are reaping what you have sown. Because we all are going to pass on into eternity when it is our time, but it was Judgment day for Pharaoh, and all of Egypt. God told Moses to go one last time and command Pharaoh to let his people go. And once again Pharaohs' heart was hardened, and he would not let them go. I believe God was hardening Pharaohs' heart to prove to Israel his love for them, and to get it through to them that they were set apart for him. In Exodus 11:4, God's word says, "And Moses said, Thus saith the Lord, about midnight will I go out into the midst of Egypt: 5. And all the firstborn in the land of Egypt shall die, from the firstborn of Pharaoh that sitteth upon his throne, even unto the firstborn of the maidservant, that is behind the mill; and all the firstborn of beasts. 6. And there shall be a great cry throughout all the land of Egypt, such as there was none like it, nor shall be like it anymore. 7. But against any of the children of Israel shall not a dog move his tongue, against man or beast: that ye may know how that the Lord doth put a difference between the Egyptians and Israel. Then in Exodus 12:3, God says to Moses, "Speak ye unto all the congregation of Israel saying, In the tenth day of this month they shall take to them every man a lamb, according to the house of their Fathers, a lamb for an house: 7. And they shall take of the blood and strike it on the two side posts and on the upper door post of the houses, wherein they shall eat it. 8. And they shall eat the flesh in that night, roast with fire, and unleavened bread; and with bitter herbs they shall eat it…11. And thus shall ye eat it; with your loins girded your shoes on your feet, and your staff in your hand; and ye shall eat it in haste: it is the Lord's Passover. 12. For I will pass through the land of Egypt this night, and will smite all the firstborn in the land of Egypt, both man and beast; and against all the gods of Egypt I will execute judgment; I am the Lord. 13. And the blood shall be to you for a token upon the houses where ye are: and when I see the blood, I will pass over you, and the plague shall not be upon you to destroy you, when I smite the land of Egypt.

"At Midnight: Give Me the Blood"

Give me the blood
when my heart is broken.
For it is a sign, you, God, will remember.
It is my only Token.

Give me the blood
when trouble hits my home.
The blood flowing from the cross.
And may from the cross I never roam.

Give me the blood,
when my finances are low.
For it's not what I know
but who I know.

And if I know Jesus
like I think I know.
He'll take care of me
for he loves me so.

Give me the blood and may every area
to my heart and life it be applied.
For it's only through the blood,
my needs he will provide.

When Judgment comes give me the blood,
to pay my sin debt.
Oh, Destroyer pass over me, may you see only the blood.
And mercy only may I get.

Give me the blood
so at midnight, I'll make it through.
For only when he sees the blood,
judgment will pass over you.

14. And this day shall be unto you for a memorial; and ye shall keep it a feast to the Lord throughout your generations; ye shall keep it a feast by an ordinance forever." Moses went out and called them for the elders of Israel and told them what the Lord told him to tell them. In Exodus 12:21-27, Moses told them to put blood on the door posts of their houses, so when the destroyer came, he would pass over them and not destroy them. So when Satan comes to try to destroy my soul, I claim the blood of Jesus!

"I Claim the Blood"

When I think, Lord
of what you did for me.
Way back upon Calvary's tree.

I'm overwhelmed with gratitude,
and I get all teary-eyed.
Because I know
for me you died.

The thorns you bore
upon your head.
And the precious blood
you shed.

Was for me,
that I could be free.
And have life
more abundantly.

The stripes you bore upon your back,
so I could have healing divine.
For because of what you did, Lord,
healing now, is mine.

I claim your blood, Lord,

just as you want me to.
For when I look at the cross,
you say, "I did that for you."

So I claim your blood, Lord.
I won't insult your Grace.
For what you did on Calvary,
for me, was not a waste.

I claim your blood, Lord,
when I have a broken heart.
For what you did on Calvary,
gave me a new start.

When my life
is full of sin.
I thank you, Lord, for Calvary.
I have peace and hope within.

So when I feel so all alone,
and there's not a friend anywhere.
you take me back to Calvary,
for I'm never alone there.

I claim your blood.
upon my soul.
For that's what
makes me whole.

For only the blood of Jesus
heals, delivers and saves.
So, Lord, I claim your blood,
to give me what my heart desperately craves.

Love, healing, hope, forgiveness,
total freedom from my sin.
I claim your blood,
and I receive your everlasting life within.

Even though God hardened Pharaohs' heart causing the Israelites (God's chosen people) to suffer. God was still in the process of delivering them. It may have looked like things were getting worse and they even said that to Moses in Exodus 6: 20-26. God was still mightily delivering them. Even though they had to go through the plagues he was in the process of delivering them. They did not actually experience the plagues like the Egyptians because God protected them. But to them it was still frightening after all they had been through before. But God was proving himself faithful to them. Too many times we forget that God is with us and we let the circumstances get us down. But we do not have to. When we know Jesus is with us we can walk through anything. Sometimes Jesus comes to us and we don't realize it is him. Our circumstances may change and we think it is the enemy of our souls. Jesus may have come to us and we didn't even realize it. With Jesus living in us we can be full of faith and walk above those troubled waters. In Matthew 14: 24-31, the disciples were out on a boat and Jesus came walking to them on the sea and they were troubled. And Jesus told them to "Be of good cheer, it is I; be not afraid. And Peter answered him and said, "Lord, if it be thou, bid me come unto thee on the water." And Jesus said unto Peter, "Come." And Peter got out of the boat and walked on the water to Jesus. But when he saw the strong wind he was afraid, he began to sink. And as he began to sink he cried, "Lord, save me!" And immediately Jesus stretched forth his hand, and caught him, and said unto him, "O thou of little faith, wherefore didst thou doubt?" And then the wind ceased. We don't have to let the problems and cares of this world bring us down. When we keep our eyes on Jesus and off of our problems we can put them under our feet. Because he has overcome, we can also!

"He's Overcome This World"

I refuse to be down
discouraged or blue.
For I know my Redeemer lives,
and he will see me through.

To grumble, complain,
murmur and gripe, I refuse.
To worship, praise and adore,
by an act of my will to do, I choose.

For though there are heartaches and trials,
in this world here, I do meet.
I will be of good cheer; my Lord lives in me,
and everything is under his feet.

Too many times we let our feelings and emotions rule us. It should not be that way. We are to rule our feelings. The Word of God says in Colossians 3:15, and let the peace of God rule in your hearts to the which also ye are called in one body; and be ye thankful. Let the Word of Christ dwell in you richly in all wisdom; teaching and admonishing one another in Psalms and hymns, and spiritual songs, singing with grace in your hearts to the Lord. And whatsoever ye do in word or deed, do all in the name of the Lord Jesus, giving thanks to God and the Father by him."

No Reason to Grumble

I have no reason to grumble
gripe, whine or live in strife.
For my Lord Jesus is with me,
and he gives me eternal life.

He is the Word that is living,

walking inside of me.
So no foe can conquer,
for God's truth is my strategy.

When the enemy comes against me,
(which he often does),
through God's Word, now faith is
and the problems are only was.

For now I'm filled with faith
if I truly believe.
God's Word covers my problems
and from them it does relieve.

So instead of panicking, grumbling or complaining when going through difficult circumstances, by an act of our will, we can choose to have faith and rejoice and praise the Lord.

I Choose to have Faith!

When the winds of change
are rocking our boat,
and we're trying everything we can
to stay afloat.

We can't let discouragement
take control.
For we have a choice
what we let in our soul.

Or we can allow God's peace
in our hearts to rule.
And we can choose to live wise,
and not live like a fool.

It is our choice
by an act of our will.
To go by God's Word
or by the way that we feel?

When it seems like our life is falling apart and Satan has brought out his "big guns" of discouragement, depression and despair we can put our hope in God.

"Put Your Hope in God"

You are hurting and you're lonely.
He is there for you!
Put your hope in God,
he will pull you through.

He will lift you up
out of the depths of despair.
Put your hope in a God
who is always there!

Put your hope in a God
who for you has a plan.
He has a purpose for you,
while living in this land.

Put your hope in Jesus
and make him your Lord.
Don't be discouraged,
for Jesus is your reward.

If you are walking through
the valley of the shadow of death.
Put your hope in Jesus
while you have your breath.

For he will take you through that valley
and lead you safely home.
So even at death's door,
there is always hope!

I don't think there is anything more devastating than the loss of a loved one. But even in death there is hope. The Word of God says in 1 Thessalonians 4: 13, "But I would not have you ignorant, brethren, concerning them which are asleep, that ye sorrow not, even as other's which have no hope. For if we believe that Jesus died and rose again, even so them also which sleep in Jesus will God bring with him. For this we say unto you by the Word of the Lord, that we which are alive and remain unto the coming of the Lord shall not prevent them which are asleep. For the Lord himself shall descend from Heaven with a shout, with the voice of the Archangel, and with the trump of God; and the dead in Christ, shall rise first: Then we which are alive and remain shall be caught up together with them in the clouds, to meet the Lord in the air; and so shall we ever be with the Lord. Wherefore comfort one another with these words."

"And so shall we ever be with our Lord"

And so shall we ever
be with our Lord.
No more strife
no more discord.

No more heartache,
crying or pain.
No longer living
with those who complain.

All will be praising
and worshipping him.
He who has delivered us

from a world of sin.

Comfort each other
with this word,
and so shall we ever
be with our Lord!

So if you are struggling,
take comfort my friend.
This world with all of its sin and strife
is very soon going to end.

So comfort each other
with this word,
"And so shall we ever
be with our Lord."

No more sorrow
crying or tears.
No more aging
through all of the years.

No more getting older
for you or me.
Forever youthful
we shall be.

So comfort each other
with this word,
"And so shall we ever
be with our Lord."

No more hunger
or dying of thirst.
For the Lord shall feed those
who have put him first.

For the Lamb who is in
the midst of the throne,
he shall feed them
and never leave them alone.

So comfort each other
with this word,
"And so shall we ever
be with our Lord."
So shall we ever
be with our Lord.

Paul tells us right there in 1 Thessalonians, "Wherefore comfort each other with this Word." Why? Because he lived in this world. He knew how hard it was. He knew the pain of persecution. He knew the heartbreak and confusion of being misunderstood and falsely accused. He knew how it felt to live in a world where he did not belong. And to have such a longing in his heart to go home. And even though Paul experienced tremendous pain and suffering while on this earth, it did not compare to the glory and the joy he is experiencing now! In 2 Corinthians 4:16-18, Paul says, "For which cause we faint not; but though our outward man is dying, yet the inward man is renewed day by day. 17. For our light affliction, which is but for a moment, worketh for us a far more exceeding and eternal weight of glory; 18. While we look not at the things which are seen, but at the things which are not seen; for the things which are seen are temporal; but the things which are not seen are eternal. In 2 Corinthians 5:1 Paul says also, "For we know that if our earthly house of this tabernacle were dissolved, we have a building of God, a house not made with hands, eternal in the Heavens. 2. For in this we groan, earnestly desiring to be clothed upon with our house which is from Heaven. 3. If so be that being clothed we shall not be found naked. 4. For we that are in this tabernacle do groan, being burdened: not for that we would be unclothed, but clothed upon, that mortality might be swallowed up of life. 5. Now he that hath wrought us for the selfsame thing is God, who also hath given unto us the earnest of the Spirit. 6. Therefore we are always confident, knowing that, whilst we are at home in the body, we are absent from the Lord: 7. (For we walk by faith, not by sight:) 8. We are confident, I say, and willing rather to be absent from the body, and to be present with the Lord." Paul was able to go through all of the suffering he experienced, because of his hope of Heaven. He walked by faith and not by sight.

"Moving by Faith"

By faith I'm moving through this land.
By faith I'm holding to the Master's hand.

By faith I'm walking not by sight.
Knowing everything's going to be all right.

For faith is the assurance of things hoped for.
Faith is the key that unlocks the door.

Faith is the evidence of things not seen.
By faith on Jesus Christ I lean.

For he's with me every day.
He leads me and guides every step of the way.

Though I can't see him I know that he's there.
By faith, he's with me every where.

By faith he's holding onto my hand.
Taking me into my Promised Land.

By faith I know my needs are supplied.
For look who is on my side.

The one who by faith framed the earth.
The one who by faith, gave every thing it's birth.

He just spoke and it was done.
So you know you can put your faith in his Son.

So have faith don't fear.
For the Lord is near.

He'll never leave though you can't see.
He will never forsake he is always nigh thee.

The word of faith is in thy mouth and in thine heart.
Just confess and believe and he will give you a new start.

He'll make you new, he'll make you whole.
By faith just let him have control.

Give him your life, give him your everything.
Lay it all down, on the altar to him bring.

Then by faith you'll be moving too.
He'll be with you in all that you do.

Then you will know it's gonna be all right.
So walk by faith and not by sight.

By faith change your world by what you say.
Tell that mountain get out of your way!

For you shall have what you believe.
So by faith wonderful things receive.

Rejoice and know they are on their way.
The answers you need, to the prayers you pray.

For God cannot lie, he will do what he said.
So don't go by sight. By faith be led.

Things will change then you will see.

By faith right now see the victory.

By faith he leads then we see.
The miracles that are coming to be.

For what we see is what we get.
So if it hasn't happened yet,

Stand firm with your faith firmly set!
Know in your heart, all needs are met.

Don't waiver or sway have faith and pray.
Thank God for what is coming your way!

Too often we go by what we see and feel in the natural. But that is not faith. God's word tells us the meaning of "faith". In Hebrews 11:1, God says, "Now faith is, the substance of things hoped for, the evidence of things not seen. For by it the Elders obtained a good testimony."

"Faith is the Substance of Things Hoped For"

See me holding you,
when you feel I'm not there.
See me holding you
when you have not a friend to share.

See at the end of the tunnel
past the dark, to the light.
See now the miracles you need.
Even though they seem no where in sight.

See past the valley
to the Mountain.
See past the dry desert
to the Fountain.

See in your life my hand
upon everything.
See in the trials
the blessings that I bring.

See now the grass is green,
and not on the other side.
See now the peace after the storm,
and after the raging tide.

See now the crown
at the end of the race.
See now I am!
Don't let anything else take my place.

See past the sky
that sometimes is gray.
See and understand, after the long night,
there is coming the day.

See already the answer
that is on the way.
Past the doubts, the questions
and the dismay.

During the trials, see now the songs
that is coming out of this.
See past the pain and heartache,
to the Heavenly Bliss.

This is the point, my child,
I don't want you to miss.
The substance of things hoped for
is what faith is!

It is all a matter of what we see. Are we looking at only what we can see in the natural? Our problems, our bills, our bad health, troubles in our relationships? Or are we looking at God and what he has done and can do? When God brought the Israelites out of Egypt you would think they would not be scared of anything. They watched their mighty God defend them and deliver them. But they came right up to the Red Sea with no where to go. There was nothing but trouble all around. They thought they were finally free from Pharaoh and the Egyptians but there they were again, breathing down their backs. What were they to do? The Egyptians behind them and water so deep and terrifying in front of them. Going by what they saw in the natural, there was absolutely no way out of their dilemma. It was all a matter of what they were looking at. When they looked at the Egyptians behind, and the water in front of them there was no way. But when they looked to God there was a way. For there is nothing impossible with God! Look to God and you shall not be moved. Seek him for he is the Way.

"I'm Not Moved By What I See"

It doesn't move me
though I see
Pharaoh's Army
chasing me.

It doesn't move me
though I see,
nothing but deep, deep water
befalling me.

It doesn't move me
if I don't know what is up ahead.
For I know God is Faithful,
and by his Spirit I am led!

He did not bring me this far,

to now watch me drown.
He's been with me every step,
and he never lets me down.

He is too good to leave me
Oh! This I know.
Especially, Especially
when I need him so!

So no matter what it looks like
with the enemy all around.
He delivered me from Egypt,
He won't leave me now, I have found.

This Red Sea almost made me forget
of his power in his mighty hand.
But my God is able to lead me,
from Egypt to my Promised Land.

To this purpose I was brought
so his power would be known.
So I'm not moved by what I see,
God's Power will be shown!

I've got to remember and never forget,
my God is the one who made that Red Sea.
That is why I know that I can trust him
to safely deliver me.

He has a way already made,
through that Red Sea for me.
So I will give him the Glory now,
and throughout all Eternity!

That is the key right there in that last sentence. So I will give him the glory now and throughout all of eternity. When we do everything for God's glory, he will move Heaven and Earth. We have to give him glory now. We can't be people who say well, I'm going to wait until I get to Heaven to praise Jesus. I'm going to wait until I get to Heaven before I live for God's glory. I'm going to wait until then to walk in faith. I will have plenty of time to worship him then. If you are one of those that is saying that right now, don't be deceived. For if you have waited until eternity you have waited one breath too late. If you are waiting for your circumstances to change before you give him the glory, then you may be waiting a long time. Sometimes we have to move forward and then our circumstances will change. And during those times we easily forget how our Lord has saved us, delivered us and protected us from the enemy. How quickly we (like the Israelites) get fearful and worried when faced with a "Red Sea" experience. You may have come to a point in your life where you know you know the Lord. You know you are his child, but it feels like the enemy is closing in on you. There may be no other choice for you but to go forward into the deep. Well! As the Lord told Moses when the Israelites were weeping about what to do, God told Moses to tell them to go forward. They had to go forward in complete faith and assurance God was going to see them through. They had to believe that God was not going to let them "down" or "drown". Sometimes we go through those "Red Sea" experiences for opportunities to prove his awesome power. It should not be a time we get all fearful and want to stop. No! That is definitely the time to go forward. Go forward in faith knowing God loves you and he is on your side! Paul says in Romans 8:31, "If God be for us, who can be against us? He that spared not his own Son, but delivered him up for us all, how shall he not with him freely give us all things?" We have to really get that down deep in our hearts. God gave his only begotten Son for each one of us, how much more with him will he freely give us all things? It does not matter what your circumstances are saying to you right now. God loves you and there is hope with him. There was a Prophet a long time ago, whose name was "Habukkuk". Habukkuk found out that he could put his hope in God. Yes, he went through problems just like we do now. But Habukkuk said, No matter what I am going to rejoice and put my hope in God. Mostly everyone God used went through trying times. Times of trouble and testing. They were no different than we are today. They were just as human as we are. But Habukkuk said in 3:17, "Although the fig tree shall not blossom, neither shall fruit be in the vines, the labour of the olive shall fail; and the fields shall yield no meat; the flock shall be cut off from the fold, and there shall be no herd in the stalls; v. 18 Yet I will rejoice in the Lord, I will joy in the God of my salvation. v. 19. The Lord God is my strength, and he will make my feet like hinds feet, (the feet of a deer), and he will make me to walk upon mine high places, to the chief singer on my stringed instruments."

"Hope Like Habukkuk"

There was a Prophet
in the bible long ago.
He had problems
like we have here below.

Things that were happening
he couldn't figure out.
He learned to trust
and got rid of that doubt.

Habukkuk said, no matter what
I will rejoice.
For my God is a good God,
I will lift my voice.

I will sing and shout
for there is hope.
For my God will strengthen
and help me to cope.

Oh! I have so much

to sing about.
Though the things I see
might make me doubt.

I'll hope yet in my God
and walk by faith.
For no matter what it looks like
My God will make a way!

No matter what the things I see,
are telling me.
I'll walk by Faith
and miracles I shall see.

So rejoice and hope in a God
that cannot fail.
For there is always hope
with God All is Well!

As Habukkuk said even though nothing seemed to be happening and things were not going right and it all appeared to be hopeless. He says in verse 18, "Yet I will rejoice in the Lord, I will joy in the God of my salvation." He chose by an act of his will to rejoice and joy in the Lord. He said, "Yet I will!" He was determined to be joyful in the Lord. He knew the Lord God was his strength. We can't let Satan use our circumstances to steal our hope and joy. For we don't want to please him. We want to please Jesus, don't we? We don't want to bring Satan any pleasure at all. See it pleases Satan when we get our eyes off of Jesus and onto our circumstances. For it is then he gets us down, discouraged and depressed. Then we are no threat to his kingdom. Satan hates us to be happy and joyful. So no matter what, hang onto your hope and joy in the Lord. For the joy of the Lord is your strength.

"Hear the Lord Speaking to You"

Don't lose your hope, don't lose your joy.
Don't let anything get you down.
For the devil loves to see you discouraged, hopeless
seeing you frown.

Don't let him have
his evil way with you.
For no matter what happens
I'll always bring you through.

No problem is too big
or hopeless that I can't solve.
No conflict, circumstance or disappointment
that I can't resolve.

For I will my sweet child
make a way for you, you will see.
Don't lose your faith
hope or joy in me!

Trust me my child
it will be all right.
You are not going under.
Don't fear, don't panic or live in fright.

Be happy, be glad
let joy fill your heart.
For my child, I am with you forever,
and we shall never, ever part!

I have had my share of hard times and the only thing that has ever kept me hanging on was hearing my Lord encouraging me. We have to hear the Lord encouraging us when we are going through difficult times. Just one word will put us over or bring us through. Just one word will mean life or death. Because sometimes we let our circumstances dictate to us how we are to be. Sometimes we go through some very painful times. Maybe even a death of a loved one. Or a divorce. Or maybe we don't know how we are going to make end's meet. It is hard to be Joyful and hopeful when going through hard times. And certainly if we have lost a loved one. No one expects you to be joyful then. However, hearing the Lord speak to us and assures us that everything is going to be all right, it makes all the difference. If you are feeling frustrated, troubled or confused maybe the Lord is trying to speak to you and you can't hear him clearly. Or you are just plainly not listening to him. Have you ever turned on the television or radio and you wanted so bad to listen to your favorite program, but it just so happens there is a lot of static at the time and you get frustrated, troubled or even aggravated. Because you want to hear what they are saying and you strain and strain. Or maybe you put your ears right up to the radio so you won't miss a thing that person is saying. Or maybe you could hear that person but there were other radio stations or t.v. programs interfering at the time. And if you could've you would have told them to be quiet you want to hear what that other person is saying. Well! Sometimes we have to do that with our Lord Jesus. We have to be determined to hear his voice. And if we want to bad enough we will strain or do whatever it takes to hear him. The Lord says in Jeremiah, "And ye shall seek me and find me when ye seek me with all of your heart." Sometimes we need to be determined with all of our heart to seek the Lord and hear his voice. So clear away the obstacles and overlook the static.

"Overlook the Static"

There may be a lot of static, clouding out what you are
trying to see and hear.
Look beyond all the static and listen hard
to what the static is trying to interfere.

Get rid of all discouragement,
fear and doubt.
Open your ears

and just shut the static out.

Past all other voices,
be determined to hear and see
past all of the static
to what is coming to be.

For the devil will have you look
at all the static that is hindering your way.
He will do anything he can
to cloud your vision to cause it to delay.

So just hang on and listen.
Before long the static will subside.
So overlook the static
and look to Jesus and in him safely abide!

Satan will try anything and everything he can to keep you from hearing the Lord speak to your heart. He will even try to get you to blame God for your problems. He will try to get you angry and offended with the Lord, so you won't even want to talk to him. He will try to make you run from the Lord instead of to him. Whatever you are going through, whether it is good or bad, always run to Jesus. Never run away from him. For he is all you need. No matter how discouraged you get or even if you get mad at God. You can confess it to the Lord and he will understand. No since in hiding it, he already knows it anyway. Don't listen to Satan trying to lure you away from the Lord. Listen to the Lord calling you into that Secret Place with him. Get alone with the Lord and shut everything and everyone out and tell the Lord how you feel in a respectful way. For he loves you and he won't get mad at you. He wants you to share your heart with him. Psalms 91:1, "As David says "He that dwelleth in the Secret Place of the most high shall abide under the shadow of the Almighty."

"Secret Place"

When the pressures get to you.
You don't know
what you are going to do.
You pray the Lord will take you home,
before the pressure finishes you.

You feel so battered
so beaten so blue.
Just wait upon the Lord
Get alone and worship him
your strength he will renew.

Years of abuse have taken their toll.
And you're so weary in your soul.
So get alone with Jesus.
On him your cares you can roll.

Though by others you've been
rejected, hurt and betrayed.
You can trust Jesus.
When on the Altar it has all been laid.

Jesus will be there.
He will never leave you nor never forsake.
And that hurt that you face, that tears you apart.
Go to Jesus, that hurt he will take!

Nothing you can do will make him love you less.
For we are saved only by his Grace.
He will mend your heart.
So get alone with him in that Secret Place!

There is a refuge, a shelter.
A secret place I can go.
To get away from the fire

from the heat that would burn me so.

ASecret Place of Refuge,
from the cold, blistering wind.
I get alone with Jesus
Oh! He's my dearest friend.

So when the enemy shoots those darts at me.
They're coming so fast, one by one.
I trust in Jesus and I hide in him,
the victory for me, he has won!

So in every battle, the Lord is my commander.
He's my sword, and my shield
I stand in faith, and hide in him.
And to him my all, I yield.

When the enemies'
big guns of discouragement
and fiery darts of fear are hurled.
I stand in that Secret Place
For Greater is He that is in me,
than he that is in the world!

There is hope in this world knowing that there is a secret place you can go when Satan shoots all his fiery darts at you. And it never occurred to me why it is called a "Secret" place. Sometimes when going through a difficult time, people are watching you to see what you are going to do. And sometimes they may wonder how can you go through what you are going through and still be standing, still be happy, still be joyful. They wonder what your secret is. See when you stay in that secret place with Jesus you can have peace in the middle of war! Jesus will give you peace to sleep like a baby. In Psalms 42:8, David says, "I will both lay me down in peace and sleep; For the Lord only makest me dwell in safety." Daniel found that out also when he was shut up in that den of hungry lions.

"Sleep On My Child"

My child though there are
troubles and trials
all around you.
Lie down in peace
and sleep on.
For I am watching
in all you do.
From night time 'til dawn.

I never, ever take
my eyes off of you.
So rest and wait
patiently for me.
I'm taking care,
of everything
your needs I do see

So don't worry and fret
or live
in fear or dread.
Just trust me
and sleep on my child,
for I know what is up ahead!

Isn't it good to know that no matter what, we can call on Jesus! He is there for us twenty-four hours a day, seven days a week, three hundred and sixty five days a year. His eyes are ever on us. One thousand, four hundred and forty minutes a day his eyes are on you! Even while you are sleeping. He is right there brushing your troubled brow. He never slumbers nor sleeps. David says in Psalms 121, "I will lift up mine eyes unto the hills, from whence cometh my help. 2. My help cometh from the Lord which made heaven and earth. 3. He will not suffer thy foot to be moved; 4. He that keepeth thee will not sleep. 5. The Lord is thy keeper; the Lord is thy shade upon thy right hand. 6. The sun shall not smite thee by day, nor the moon by night. 7. The Lord shall preserve thee from all evil, he shall preserve thy soul. 8. The Lord shall preserve thy going out and thy coming in from this time forth, and even for evermore.

"He Keeps Me!"

Sometimes when I'm feeling frightened,
along this narrow way.
Battles come, storms arise,
trials darken my day.

Pressures mount, dreams vanish
right before my eyes.
I wonder sometimes how I've made it,
but really it is no surprise.

For my sweet Jesus is always, always
by my side.
The times I've felt so low
and just wanted to hide.

His mighty power to me
he doth show.
The times I haven't had any strength
and another step I just could not go.

My sweet Jesus picks me up.
I'm so glad him I know.
For he keeps me by his grace,
to him I lift up my soul. and seek
his marvelous face.

On him, my burdens I do roll.

He keeps me, he's faithful.
He'll not let me be lost.
For us my sweet Jesus
has paid a very priceless cost.

He'll keep me
until the end.
For he is my friend.

He's bought me, I'm his.
He has set me free.
So I'll not worry, nor fear.
For my Jesus keeps me!

Jesus is a good shepherd that takes excellent care of his sheep. In John 10:14 Jesus says, "I am the Good shepherd and know my sheep, and am known of mine." ·Jesus never takes his eyes off of his sheep. He takes care of their every need. When I was a little girl I had to memorize Psalms 23 and recite it in front of the whole church, just to show what I was learning in Sunday School. I did not realize until I was twenty eight years old, what that Psalms really meant. I mean I quoted it perfectly as a little girl, but it did not mean anything to me personally until I was in my late twenties. I received Jesus Christ as my Savior at the age of twelve. But did not realize until later on that he wanted to be "Lord" of my life. I did not realize until later on that I had strayed from the Lord like a little, lost lamb and I needed a Shepherd. But Jesus found me now I can say like David, The Lord is -

"My Shepherd Personally"

My Shepherd cares so much about me.
When I go and get tangled with a lot of debris.
He comes and lovingly sets me free.

He wasn't angry

He still loved me when I was astray.
Oh! When I was lost, he left the ninety and nine,
and searched for me, he went out of his way.

My Shepherd knows
how to take care of all of my needs.
He doesn't let me go hungry.
If I stay near him, me, he always feeds.

Just knowing he's holding me,
I can rest peaceful, in my shepherd's arms.
I don't have to fret,
because he will protect me, safe from all alarms.

He will keep me safe and secure
this I know without a doubt.
For he's my shepherd, I'm just a little lamb.
He doesn't ever let me do without.

My Shepherd tells me, there are wolves in the pasture.
So I better beware.
They are all around us, they are everywhere!

If I lean on my Shepherd,
from these hungry wolves, he will protect.
And the slightest bit of harm he will detect.
He anoints me with oil,
to guard me from every enemy, every insect.

He leads me,
safely up the mountainside.
He carries me when my strength is gone,
and in his bosom I do hide.

He leads me sometimes
around a treacherous cliff.
I have to depend, trust and obey.

I have to listen close to his voice.
For he is leading me every step of the way.

Often my Shepherd leads me
around the clefts of the rock.
I have to keep my eyes on my Shepherd
not on the other sheep
or the hindrances in the way that doth block.

For my Shepherd will remove
everything in my path.
Anything or anyone
that hurts his little sheep
they better fear his wrath.

For my Shepherd is always watching
he doesn't slumber nor sleep.
I don't ever have to worry,
for me, he doth keep.

My Shepherd always
guards me continually with his eye.
Through the pastures
through the valleys or on the Mountain high.

I trust him
to take care of me
to lead me and be my guide.
For my Shepherd loves me
and always wants me
close by his side!

We have to come to a point like David said, "The Lord is my Shepherd." Psalms 23, "The Lord is my Shepherd I shall not want. 2. He maketh me to lie down in green pastures He leadeth me beside the still waters. 3. He restoreth my soul; he leadeth me in the paths of righteousness for his names sake. 4. Yea, though I walk through the valley of the shadow of death, I will fear no evil; for thou art with me; thy rod and thy staff they comfort me. 5. Thou preparest a table before me in the presence of mine enemies; thou anointest my head with oil; my cup runneth over. 6. Surely goodness and mercy shall follow me all the days of my life and I will dwell in the house of the Lord for ever."

"My Shepherd"

I love you Lord.
You are the Good Shepherd.
Help me stay close to you,
All of my days.
Help me follow you in everything I do.
Guide me and keep me in all of my ways.

Help me remember and never forget,
how much you love me.
For me you've paid the cost.
Light my way, help me see,
without you as my shepherd,
I am totally lost.

I'm so glad
you are my Shepherd
For you take such awesome care of me.
For you Love me too much
to ever let me be.

David realized he had the Lord. He had all he needed. He realized he was not in control, but the Lord was his Shepherd. And David was comforted by his Shepherd's rod and staff. When he started to get away from the Sheepfold, he was glad when his Shepherd used his rod and his staff to grab ahold of him and pull him back in. He knew his Shepherd loved him and was taking care of him. He knew he was helpless without him. He knew his Shepherd was good to him. He had total confidence in the goodness of his Shepherd. He said surely goodness and mercy shall follow me all the days of my life and I will dwell in the House of the Lord forever! See he knew his shepherd was not a mean, hateful, cruel Shepherd that ruled him with an iron rod. He found out his Shepherd was loving, kind and gentle. Have you ever asked Jesus to be your Shepherd? Do you know what it means to have him care for you like you were a lost little lamb but is now found? If you do know him as your Shepherd, rest assured he is taking care of you, carrying you, leading you, guiding you and guarding you with his eye. If you don't know what it means to know the Lord as your Shepherd, all you have to do is realize that you are a lost little lamb in need of his gentle care. And ask him to be your Shepherd, your Lord, your Savior. He is waiting with open arms to be that for you right now! Trust Him! I don't know what has happened in your life. You may be feeling all beat up, battered and abused. And you may be scared to trust the Lord. You may have gotten beat up, mauled, battered and abused by a pack of wolves (so to speak). People you have trusted may have hurt you and done things to you that have left you feeling confused, hurt and abandoned. And you may be scared and thinking the Lord will do that to you also. I can assure you the Lord will never, ever hurt you. He is not angry at you. He is not waiting for you to come to him so he can clobber you with his big rod and staff. Oh! No! He loves you so much! He just wants to take care of you. He has been searching for you. Luke 15:4, Jesus says, "What man of you having an hundred sheep, if he lose one of them, doth not leave the ninety and nine, in the wilderness, and go after that which is lost until he find it? 5. And when he hath found it, he layeth it on his shoulder's rejoicing. 6. And when he cometh home, he calleth together his friends, and neighbors, saying unto them rejoice with me; for I have found my sheep which was lost." So wherever you are, trust the Lord to take care of you. Repeat this poem and mean it with all of your heart and Jesus will pick you up and carry you, rejoicing back into the sheepfold.

"Gentle Shepherd of the Field"

Gentle Shepherd
of the field.
pick me up and carry me,
for my whole self to you, I yield.

Lead me and guide me
in the direction
that I should take.
For you are the Good Shepherd of the field.
I know, me, Lord,
you will never forsake.

For you know
I'm just a little sheep
in need of your tender care.
I know not what to do
or where to go,
without you being there.

I am a lost sheep
feeble and lonely
and needing your Shepherd's arms.
So please pick me up
and carry me,
to be free from all alarms.

For there are many things
out in this field
to be afraid of.
So Lord, help me rest and help me know,
I'm in the care
of your Gentle Shepherd's Love!

Lord I give you my life and I thank you for taking care of me. I could not make it without you Lord Jesus. Thank you for loving me and thank you for forgiveness of sins. And for washing me clean with your precious blood. I could not make it without you, Lord!

"What Would I Do Without My Lord?"

What would I do without my Lord?
Guiding me along the way?
What would I do without my Lord,
Leading me from day to day?

What would I do without my Lord
holding my hand?
I'd fall off of the cliffs
I'd sink in the sinking sand.

What would I do without my Lord,
watching over me?
I'd be so lost, lonely
bound and tormented wanting to be free.

What would I do without my Lord?
I'd live in torment and fear,
day after day,
Year after year.

I thank the Lord I now have him,
and my cries he doth hear.
He's with me now,
no longer to live in torment and fear.

No more
to be lost and lonely.
No more in the sinking sand.
No more bound but free.

All because my Jesus lives, I live
and he's given me his word.
He will never leave me.
Oh! What would I do without my Lord?

I'm so glad I know Jesus! I am glad to know he loved me first before I knew him. And he drew me to him. John says in 1 John 4:10, "Herein is love, not that we loved God, but that he loved us and sent his Son to be the propitiation for our sins. Isn't it good to know God loves us, unconditionally? He loved us first! God initiated our relationship with him first. When I was running from him, scared of him, scared to run to him and scared to live without him. I am so thankful that he understood me and somehow he still got ahold of my heart

"You Got A Hold Of My Heart"

Down may roads
and down every dead end,
out in the darkness, and out in sin.
There you were
with outstretched arms
standing once again.

I was dirty and filthy

and very unclean.
I was hateful
spiteful and downright mean.

I'd run and run
for I couldn't understand why,
though very often
to figure out, I'd try.

How someone like you, Lord,
could ever love me so?
I couldn't understand,
how could you, all my burdens even know?

You said, my child, I bought you
with a price a long time ago.
Then you said to me (when I finally listened),
all my burdens on the cross did go.

All you have to do is accept it, you told me,
then my heart did melt.
Oh! The joy in my soul,
Such joy I have never, ever felt.

For when you said
those things to me,
for finally, finally
I was free, free, free!

When I seen the love and compassion in your eyes
nothing else mattered.
I didn't care anymore of hurts in the past,
of broken promises, dreams all shattered.

For when I met you Lord Jesus,
time stood still.
I gave you everything,

heart, body, mind and will.

Oh! I thank you Lord,
for never giving up on me.
Thank you for your grace
and love, you give so generously.

You'd tell me you began a good work
and you always finish what you start.
So Thank you precious Lord for:
"Getting A Hold of My Heart!"

Paul says in 2 Corinthians 5:17, "Therefore if any man be in Christ, he is a new creature; old things are passed away; behold all things are become new, I heard a phrase that said, "I'm not what I want to be, but thank God I'm not what I used to be." I thank God that he finishes what he starts Paul says in Philippians 1:6, "Being confident of this very thing, he who hath begun a good work in you shall perform it until the day of the Lord Jesus Christ."

"Not Finished With Me Yet!"

If I do something,
and with me,
you just don't agree.
Don't judge me too harshly,
for Jesus isn't finished with me yet,
you gotta see!

He's still working
on this old,
lump of clay.
He will be
still working,
until that wonderful day.

He calls me home
to my mansion
he is building for me.
So if with me you don't agree,
don't judge me too harshly,
Jesus is not finished with me, You gotta see!

Just as Jesus isn't finished with me yet. He is not through with you either! As Paul says in Philippians 1:6 "Being confident of this very thing he who hath started a good work in you will perform it until the day of the Lord Jesus Christ." Jesus always finishes what he starts.

"Not Through"

You may feel
all alone and forsaken.
You may live with regret,
of wrong steps you have taken.

You may feel down
and full of fear and dread.
You wish you wasn't even born,
to others you've often said.

You may wonder what is the use,
of even going on?
You've lost everything,
and things have gone so wrong.

You may question your very purpose,
and your reason to be.
Please remember, God has a plan
for each of us, you and me.

A plan for good, to give us
an expected end.
So you see no matter how bad,
you think it is, my friend,

and you think it is all over,
well, please think again.
For Jesus loves you,
and it is not for you the end.

For God says, "He's not through!"
He started a good work in your heart,
and he always finishes,
everything he does start.

So don't live your life
any longer with fear and regret.
Keep your faith in Jesus,
He's not finished with you yet!

Don't give up when the circumstances may be telling you "It's All Over!" For it is not over until the Lord says so!

"It's Not Over!"

You know it may look like it's all over.
That there is no way your needs will be met.
But just hang on,
it is not over, not over yet!

There may be what you thought a period
like at the end of a sentence in your situation.
But don't you forget who you know,
to who you are in relation.

For God is your Father,
and it is not over, until he says so!
So clear your eyes look again, it's not a period
but a comma, this I do know!

For Jesus is the Resurrection and the life.
So no matter what, just believe.
For Jesus opens doors to the miracles you need.
Trust Him, you will receive.

So when it looks like a period it's over.
Jesus has the keys to open that door.
He will turn it into a comma,
and get the glory forever more!

Don't let the enemy of your soul (Satan) tell you it is all over for you. It is not over! Yes, it is hard in this world sometimes and Satan just wants you to say forget it all. And he will try to make you bitter. But instead of allowing trials to make you bitter, allow them to make you better. Trust God that he knows what is going on. He knows where you are at. Don't get bitter and hard toward him. For he is the potter, and we are the clay. Keep soft and pliable in his hands. And you will be amazed at what he makes out of your life.

"Make it or Break it"

I watched a vessel being molded,
by a potter one day.
I talked with the potter of what he was doing.
Here is what he had to say.

He said I take this clay and hold it,
with oh! such tender care.
I hold it in my hands,
and it's not going anywhere.

The Potter said, "I mash it,
and I squeeze it,
and it changes
bit by bit."

The Potter knows what he is doing
he's a master at his art.
He knows how to handle the clay
every single part.

The Potter knows
exactly what to do.
He knows just how much pressure
to take the clay through.

He knows how much the clay
can stand the flame in the fire.
He knows what is good, for the vessel
and how much heat it doth require.

He keeps working on the vessel,
after he does begin.
He keeps his eyes upon it.
Never to take them off again.

To make it or break it and shape it,
into a beautiful design.
And then he puts his name upon it,
and says this work of art is mine!

What an awesome thought, God is molding and shaping us into something grand. Even though it may be painful. There is no better place to be, than in the Master's hand. I would rather be in the potter's hand and go through trial's. Being pounded, molded, shaped, spinned and put in the fire, than to be on my own and not go through anything. And not grow spiritually. Or I'd rather be out in the deep in the middle of a storm with Jesus than to be out on the shore in the sunshine without him. And that does not mean that we are not in our Lord's hands if we haven't gone through any trials. What I mean is I would not trade any of the trials I have had for a life of ease and pleasure. All of the trials and all of the heartaches I've had have just helped me depend on my potter the Lord Jesus Christ, all the more. For there has never, ever been a heartache or trial that my Lord has not turned it around for my good and his glory. Whatever you are going through right now, whatever trouble or heartache you are experiencing, give it to Jesus and he will use it for your good and his glory. Now I didn't say you would be exempt from suffering, but nothing the devil throws at us will succeed. It may look like he is succeeding but he is not. God is in control! And whatever you are going through it is not in vain. Give it to Jesus and he will turn it around for your good and his glory. Nothing Satan throws at a child of God can harm him. I mean it may hurt us for a moment but it can never harm us.

"Heartaches Are Blessings In Disguise"

Thank You, Lord,
for being my guide.
And thank you, Lord,
for never leaving my side.

You've been right there with me.
Through good times and bad.
Through happy times and sad.

And through joy or sorrow.
And when I go to sleep,
I don't have to worry about tomorrow.

And if some heartache or trouble arise,
it says in your word, Lord,
a broken heart you will not despise.
And help us see heartaches

are blessings in disguise.

Transforming us to be,
more like you, Lord.
And teaching us,
to live by your word.

I was pondering one day after going through something else that broke my heart. I thought, "Why doesn't Satan just leave me alone? Hasn't he realized yet that he is not in control? Doesn't he know that I'm going to cry out to the Lord all the more? And I was thinking hasn't he figured it out yet? And I was thinking he is sure wasting his time, he knows his time is short, so why doesn't he just leave me alone? And the thing is, he doesn't leave us alone because he knows Jesus never leaves us alone. So he thinks that if he can keep on at us just maybe we would leave Jesus alone. He tries to get us angry and bitter at God. That is one of his motives. He did that with Job. Job was a righteous man. So much so, that God trusted him. God bragged on Job to Satan. And Satan said Job was only righteous and blessed because God had a hedge around him, and his family. Satan said to God if you take away that hedge of protection, Job would curse you to your face. God had faith in Job. He knew Job would still believe in him and love him no matter what. So God told Satan, Okay, do what you want to him, but take not his life. God allowed Satan to take his children, his health, everything except his unbelieving wife. All in one day. Could it be when we go through trials that God brags about us to Satan like he did with Job? Just to prove to Satan that we Love him not necessarily because of what he is doing for us, but simply because of who he is and because we just love him because of who he is. Maybe Satan tells Jesus we only worship God because of what God gives us. Satan may tell God, "They're not worshipping you out of love, Jesus, come on, they are only serving you out of greed and covetousness. Thinking they are going to get something back." I don't know about you but if that conversation really goes on between Jesus and Satan over me, I want to prove Jesus right! I want Jesus and Satan to know perfectly clear I'm serving Jesus out of love for him, nothing else. Don't you? Sometimes it does seem like God's hedge of protection is no longer around us. What do we do in situations like that? What do we do when it seems like we are struggling and struggling and we can't figure out why? Maybe you are going through financial trouble. Or trouble with your spouse or children? Or struggles on your job? Do you grumble and complain and get mad at God? Do you accuse God of not loving you anymore? Do you curse God and say if this is the way it is I am not going to serve you any longer? Or do you like Job did say, "Though he slay me yet I will trust him?" Satan spake through Job's wife even to get him to curse God and die, but all Job had left was God. Job knew that every thing else was passing away. And all he needed was God. Job says in Job 19:25, "For I know that my Redeemer liveth, and that he shall stand at the latter day upon the earth: 26. And though after my skin worms destroy this body, yet in my flesh shall I see God; 27. When I shall see for myself and mine eyes shall behold within me." See Job knew his God was alive! And he knew that those trials were passing on this earth or whenever he died and seen God face to face. All that mattered to him was God. Job knew that there was an end to all his suffering. For he said, "I know that my Redeemer liveth, and that he shall stand at the latter day upon the earth." James 5:11 says, "Behold, we count them happy which endure. Ye have heard of the patience of Job. And have seen the end of the Lord; that the Lord is very pitiful, and of tender mercy." There came a time when the Lord told Satan that's enough! There came a time in Job's life that along with all that suffering, there was God's comfort. God does not leave us without comfort. Though there may be many a sorrow, rejoice. Because there is also many a Comfort.

"Many a Sorrow, Many a Comfort"

Many a teardrop
Many a Heartache
Only my Lord knows
Many a Sorrow

Many a Crying
from many earthly blows

But many a tear wipe
many a comfort
words can never tell
Many a hug
Many of God's Love
assuring all is well!

Just like Job experienced God's comfort and care in a way he never knew. We also experience God's Love and comfort which we would not know any other way. Had we not gone through all the trials and heartaches we've gone through we would not know first hand God's comfort. None of us want to go through trials and heartache. But we need to realize there is a purpose for our good that these trials are not in vain. Then we can give thanks in every situation.

"In Everything Give Thanks!"

Without the Thorns- I wouldn't appreciate
The Rose.
Without the Bad- I wouldn't appreciate
The Good.
Without my Loneliness- I wouldn't appreciate.
A Friend.
Without the Rain- I wouldn't appreciate
The Sun.
Without the Prison- I wouldn't appreciate
My Freedom.
Without the Trials- I wouldn't appreciate
The Blessings.
Without My Questions- I wouldn't appreciate
God's Wisdom.
Without the Dark- I wouldn't appreciate
The Light.

Without the Sorrow- I wouldn't appreciate
Joy.
Without the Valley- I wouldn't appreciate
The Mountain.
Without the Race- I wouldn't appreciate
The Goal.
Without the Fight- I wouldn't appreciate
The Prize.
Without My Weakness- I wouldn't appreciate
God's Strength.
Without My Helplessness- I wouldn't appreciate
God's Help!

Sometimes it takes the hard times, the struggles, the weaknesses we go through, to make us appreciate what God offers us. Often when going through upsetting circumstances where people I have loved did not agree with me. I would often say to my Lord, "Boy I sure am glad you love me, Lord, because I don't feel like anyone else does. Then I would tell him I could not make it without his love. Because sometimes it has seemed like he was my only friend. Now don't get me wrong, I do know a lot of people. But knowing a lot of people and being assured that they really love you and are there for you through thick or thin, are two different things. You can be very popular and have many people around you all of the time and still be very lonely. But that's okay because when we wake up and realize that we are lonely, it is then that we appreciate the fact that Jesus is with us always. Had it not been for my loneliness I wouldn't have appreciated God. I probably would have taken him for granted. Paul knew how that felt also. Paul says in 2 Corinthians 12:5-10, that he would not glory about himself, about his accomplishments or his abilities. But he would only glory in his weakness. Paul gave thanks even for his weakness, because it made him appreciative of God's strength. He knew he was nothing without God. Paul learned to Thank God for the thorns for it made him appreciative of the rose. For he says in v.7 "Lest I should be exalted above measure through the abundance of the revelations, there was given to me a thorn in the flesh, the messenger of Satan to buffet me, lest I should be exalted above measure." Then Paul says, "I sought the Lord three times that it might depart from me." And each time the Lord told him, v.9 "My Grace is sufficient for thee, for my strength is made perfect in weakness." Then Paul said, "Most gladly therefore will I rather glory in my weakness, that the power of Christ may rest upon me." Paul was able to thank God for the thorns. Like on a rose, because of thorns they make the "rose" part of the whole flower so much more enjoyable.That part of the whole flower we call a rose is more appreciated. Paul was not puffed up in pride, because of that "thorn" it kept him humble and appreciative. When Jesus met Paul on that road to Damascus, he was changed! He knew now who was in control, and he didn't mind it at all. All he wanted was to please Jesus and live for his glory. It didn't matter about the thorns. It didn't matter to him what people said or did to him. It did not matter how much their words and actions pierced his soul. He knew that there was a rose along with them thorns. He recognized that he also knew that he was weak. Only until we come to see our weakness and our helplessness, will we appreciate God's strength and help in time of need. It is such an Honor and privilege to be able to go to God and cry out to him and be able to tell him our weaknesses, and our helplessness without him turning his nose down to us. No! He doesn't do that. People may do that to us. But Jesus will never do that. Sometimes our own family members cannot tolerate our helplessness or our weaknesses, but Jesus can. Often people want us around when we are doing well. But then when we need help from others, they tend to point their noses down to us. There is a story in the bible in Luke 7:36. It's about Jesus went to this man's home, whose name was Simon. And as he was sitting there eating, a lady in that city who did not have a very good reputation came running into the house. And she knelt down at Jesus' feet and weeping she poured oil from an alabaster box, onto his feet and began wiping his feet with her hair. And Simon was only thinking in his heart, "Lord if you only knew what manner of woman this is, you wouldn't let her touch you. And Jesus looked at him, for Jesus knew his thoughts. And he said, "Simon, I have somewhat to say against thee, and Jesus began telling him a parable and said, "There was a certain creditor which had two debtors; the one owed two hundred and twenty dollars and and the other twenty two dollars. 42. And when they had nothing to pay, he frankly forgave them both. Tell me therefore which of them will love him most? Verse 43. says, "Simon answered and said, "I suppose that one to whom he forgave the most. And Jesus said, "Thou hast rightly said,. v. 44 And he returned to the woman and said unto Simon, "Seest thou this woman? I entered into thine house, thou gave me no kiss; but this woman hath anointed my feet with ointment. 47. Wherefore I say unto thee; Her sins which are many are forgiven for she loved much; but to whom little is forgiven the same loveth little, and he said unto her, "Thy sins are forgiven." That lady realized her need for Jesus! Because she realized her weakness she was able to depend on the Lord Jesus for strength. She heard of Jesus then she found out where he was at. Simon sat right there with Jesus but he took him for granted and he didn't realize his need for him. His self righteousness caused him to judge that Lady. No he may not have done the things this lady had done, but he still needed Jesus, just as well as she did. I'm sure he was proud to have Jesus come to eat with him, because he was so good. Because he thought within himself if Jesus knew what kind of woman this was Jesus would not have even let her touch him. He probably worried what others would say.Simon sat right there in the presence of Jesus but yet did not connect heart to heart with Jesus like that woman did.There are many today like Simon. Who may sit every Sunday on a church pew. But they are going to be left behind when Jesus returns, if they don't connect with Jesus heart to heart. Simon did not have a love relationship with Jesus. He only invited Jesus into his house to make his own "self" look better. We have to repent of pride and get self off of the throne of our hearts and let Jesus rule there. Repent of pride and realize you are nothing and have nothing if you are not totally relying on Jesus Christ for everything you have and are, even for your very breath. And God will give you Grace. He will grace you with his very presence. Remember he resists the proud but giveth grace to the humble. Jesus says in Luke 14:11, "For whosoever exalteth himself shall be humbled, and he that humbleth himself shall be exalted. This woman found forgiveness because she saw her need, and humbled herself before the Lord. She wasn't depending on herself because she knew she was a sinner. Simon and no-one else needed to tell her that. In Psalms 40:4 David says, "Blessed is the man that maketh the Lord his trust, and respecteth not the proud, nor such as turn aside to lies." Simon was trusting in himself that he was good. But that woman came in and solely was putting her trust in the goodness and mercy of the Lord. And the Lord respected her! When no-one else gave her respect. Our Lord Jesus did. Have you ever had Jesus tell you he respected you? What an awesome thing. We need to ask ourselves, Are we like Simon or are we like that sinner woman? Are we trusting in ourselves that we are good and righteous? Or do we, or have we seen our need for Jesus? And are we totally depending on God's Grace and Mercy? Are we trusting in the Lord for strength and confidence from him?

"Her Strength is In Jesus"

She grew up in a Home
not knowing what love meant.
She never had a hug,
her life was Hell bent.

She didn't know why
she was born twenty one years ago.
She often questioned why,
her life was so.

'Til she met her true love
at a church where she did go.
Now true Love
she does know!.

She felt so much love
when she walked through the door.
It was there. It was then.
She met her Lord. She met her Savior.

She met him at the altar

while on her knees.
He seen her pain, he seen her tears,
he heard her desperate pleas.

Now she knows it doesn't matter
about the past anymore.
For he has made all things new,
they are not like before.

He's given her a reason
to rejoice and be glad.
Now she's receiving more love,
than she's ever had.

Now everyone knows
where her strength lies.
in the good times and bad times,
in the lows and highs.

Her strength is in Jesus
the lover of her soul.
She's complete in him now.
He's who makes her whole.

Her strength lies in Jesus
who can never fail.
He's who saved her,
from an Eternity in Hell.

Her strength is in Jesus
though she's weak, he is strong.
Though she's had hard times,
he's given her a song.

Her strength is in Jesus
she walks with him all day.
Traveling on a Journey

up the narrow way.

Her strength is in Jesus
her true Love.
Until he comes and takes her,
to their home above.

She lives for him each day now,
with all of her heart.
She is to him so thankful
for her new start.

He's given her the hope
to go on from day to day.
Her strength lies in Jesus
No matter what comes her way.

There is Hope for all of us today. When we like that Sinner woman in Luke 5 come to the realization we are hopeless, without him. When we come to see our need for him, our helplessness, and our weaknesses, then and only then will we appreciate his help and his strength. Simon did not come to that realization yet. He sat right there in the presence of Jesus. He wasn't thankful nor appreciative for Jesus coming to eat with him that day. After all he was a "good" person. That was the least Jesus could do, so he thought. But Jesus knew beforehand what was going to happen that day. He had an appointment with that woman. He knew she was going to show up. I'll just deal with Simon's self-righteousness while she's here also. He loved that sinner woman also and he knew she was going to show up. His love drew her there that day. His Love opened his eyes up to her need for him.

"Now She Knows Love!"

She grew up in a home
all scared and lonely.

in a small Kentucky town
she grew to be.
A woman on her own
Now pushing Forty.
She asks herself,
"What is there here for me?"

She wanted so bad for someone,
who really understood.
She looked so hard to find,
but no-one ever could.

She spent most of her life
in heartache and pain.
Every Love she had abused her.
She lived her life in vain.

She knew in her heart
there was a longing.
For something better
to ease her suffering.

She remembers
someone telling her of Jesus.
As a Teen
one day on an old school bus.

She remembers that they told her
that he loved her.
And things didn't have to be
like they were.

That Jesus would for her
make thing's new again.
That he would forgive
and take away her sin.

So she humbly bowed
her knee in prayer.
Hoped she would
find him there.

And she called on him
to save her.
He was there
and he touched her heart for sure.

She didn't worry anymore about the changes
and the wrinkles on her face.
For that day when she called on Jesus,
something happened at that place.

All the hurt in her past
he did erase.
For she was born again, made new,
by his precious Grace.

She was a "new creature
in Christ Jesus".
Because of a friend,
on an old school bus.

Who she remembered,
shared with her the Gospel.
Who was kind and loving,
and not ashamed to tell.

Now she knows Love,
more than she could ever imagine.
For she called on Jesus,
and he washed away her sin.

God's Word says, "Faith cometh by hearing and hearing by the Word of God." Just like that woman in Luke 5, she heard Jesus was at Simon's house, and she ran to him. I too, like that lady heard about Jesus, and I knew I needed him. I cried out to him one day at the end of my road and he heard me.

"He Heard My Cry!"

I was going down
a sinful road,
full of pain and misery.
I thought it was, absolutely,
the end for me.

'Til I cried out to Jesus
he came and rescued me.
When others turned away.
Oh! He heard me.

Oh! He heard my cry,
of despair and distress.
He reached down and picked me up,
and now my soul's at rest.

He didn't turn away from me.
And he didn't cast me out.
Now because he heard me.
I now sing and shout.

Oh! Glory Hallelujah.
He's so good and kind.
For since he answered my cry.
New Life in Him I find.

Oh! He heard my cry
of despair and distress.

He reached down and picked me up.
And now my soul is at rest!

It took me going down that road of loneliness and pain, before I seen my need of Jesus. It took the darkness to make me appreciate him who is the light. There was a time when going through problems. I tried to make it on my own. I told the Lord basically to leave me alone. I wanted what I wanted and that was that! I wanted to go on my own way. And the Lord being a gentleman that he is, let me go. Little did I know what was in store for me. It was a life of torment, loneliness, darkness, pain and despair. A life of confusion, emptiness, hurt and sorrow. But it took all those things to make me call on Jesus. Now I appreciate Jesus and his grace and mercy. I thank God that he loves me and I thank him so much for a second chance. And for years Satan tried to make me believe Jesus didn't love me any longer, because I turned my back on him. But he is a liar. And Jesus helped me and took me back. So if you are out there today reading this and you may have turned your back on the Lord and left home like the Prodigal son in Luke 15. Don't listen to the lies of the enemy telling you, that you can't go back home again, "For you can go home again."

"You Can Go Home Again!"

Out in the darkness
and out in the distance.
I was living such a wasted life.
I longed for my old home,
but I had so much resistance.

For you see I had a neighbor,
who did not want me to return.
And every time I tried, he wouldn't let me go.
He didn't want me the truth to learn.

About my old home and family

he would often tell me lies.
Though at the time,
just lies they were, though I didn't realize.

He would always tell me
my family would not ever take me back.
He would tell me I was a forever hopeless, lost sheep,
and I was the only one black.

He would tell me,
my Father did not even remember me.
I was forever forgotten,
and to let my old family be.

But in my heart
the hunger and desire,
just would not go away.
It grew and grew and grew
each passing day.

I kept thinking
about my Father,
and all that I left behind.
I couldn't quit thinking about being home.
It just would not leave my mind.

My neighbor kept telling me,
to forget it, the place in my home,
I had before, I would never again find.
And the more I listened to him,
I became more and more blind.

He kept on and on and on.
And just would not let me be.
I was feeling so lost and helpless,
and from this neighbor I just wanted to be free.
For the more I lived near this neighbor

I realized he wasn't really a kind neighbor at all.
But really my enemy.

Then one bright and glorious morning,
a new neighbor moved in nearby.
My old neighbor didn't want me to meet him,
and I could not figure out why.

So I got bound and determined
this old neighbor was not going
any longer to run my life.
So I pressed on
to my new neighbor
and went and told him, Hi!

He told me it was me anyhow
that he was looking for.
He was a friend of my Father's.
He came to find me and take me back home
to where I was at before.

I was so thankful and overjoyed,
I couldn't even speak.
For just a moment before
my heart was so heavy so burdened, so bound, so weak.

I had been around,
that old neighbor, for oh! so long.
The hold he had on me.
I didn't realize for it was very, very strong.

I'm so glad I met
this new neighbor of mine
and he came to my rescue.
I feel so happy,
so clean so refreshed, so new.

I'd like to tell you,
what has happened since then.
I'm glad to say my old neighbor,
did not have his way.
Me and my new neighbor
are going back home this day.

My old neighbor was a liar,
and he didn't win.
So you see no matter,
how far away from home you've been,
"You Can Go Home Again!"

Wherever you have been, wherever you are at right now, there is hope! Stop listening to the lies of Satan telling you it is no use, it is hopeless. For with God there is hope. With God there is Mercy. With God there is Forgiveness. Get tired and fed up with listening to the lies of Satan (the old neighbor) and listen to Jesus (your new neighbor). For Satan will only destroy you. He is not your friend! Stop running from Jesus, and run to Him!

"No More Running"

I look back on my life,
and see how foolish I've been
I'd run from the Lord,
living in sin.

All the guilt and the pain
was getting too much for me to bear.
Jesus was there
the whole time saying, child I care.

There is not a creature anywhere,
that is not manifest in my sight.
Step out of the dark
and into my marvelous light.

Then tired of running
I came to the end of my rope.
With all of life's problems
I could not cope.

I said, Lord forgive me for the mess,
I've made of my life.
Please, help me Lord,
and take away the strife.

Then he looks at me with loving eyes,
and says, "It is done, you are free!"
I said, "Thank you, Lord,
for your Grace and Mercy, you have given me.

Now I'll no longer,
run and hide.
For it's close by you, Lord Jesus,
I'll always abide!"

It took the Lord letting me go on for awhile in my own stubborn, sinful ways. Until I came to the point I could not go on any longer. In his grace and mercy he let me go until I got sick of the darkness. But let me point out to you if you ever hear his voice, Obey Him! Don't just think necessarily, well, I can sin presumptuously and the Lord will always take me back. What I am saying is, Don't take him for granted! He loves you! With me I had to stay in the darkness, because I turned my back on him. He let me go, and yes he did give me another chance. But I almost lost my mind in all that darkness. And what I mean when I say darkness is, I was so hopeless, so empty, nothing at all to look forward to. And I knew I was on my way to Hell! I knew about Hell. I knew I turned my back on Jesus, my only way to Heaven. So where else was I going to go, but Hell? God let me go until he knew I was absolutely sick of living my life without him. He wanted me to really realize how my life is without him. And finally when I really, really meant business with him, I called out to him and cried out to him, and he heard me and carne to me. He took me out of darkness and put me in his light. If he had not come to me when he did I would have either killed myself or been in the mental ward. I was at the end of my last dead end road. So wherever you are at God loves you and there is hope. Now I can say thank God for the dark times. For it has made me very appreciative of God's light. For he pulled me out of darkness and put me in his light.

"There Shall Be Light"

Though there are sorrows
and many troubles all around.
We can't forget,no matter what it looks like,
his Grace doth abound.

For from the creation of time
there was nothing at all but void and darkness.
And then God spoke let there be light,
So I don't care how bad something looks.

God can and will make it all right.

For God says, if we just call on the Lord,
to be saved we shall.
So no matter the hard times, just call on Jesus.
He's our way out of Hell!
Call on Jesus, trust in Him.
Then no matter what all shall be well!

We all travel this road of life, but not all of us are going the same way. Truth is, there are two roads to take. One is the broad way that leads to destruction, And the other is the straight road that leads to Heaven. Jesus says in Matthew 7:13, "Enter ye in at the straight gate; For wide is the gate, and broad is the way that leadeth to destruction, and many there be which go in thereat. v.14. Because straight is the gate, and narrow is the way, which leadeth unto life, and few there be that find it." On both roads there are storms, obstacles, valleys, mountains, highways, turns, bumps, and potholes. But one road we travel all alone, trying to figure our own way down that road. Living life with no direction, no purpose, no plan, no compass, no flashlight, no gas in our tanks, no speedometer. Going fast when we feel like it, going slow when we feel like it. Doing our own thing. No destination. No meaning. No oil keeping our engine lubricated and running. In other words there is no oil of anointing on that road to keep us going. We'll be spitting and sputtering and struggling just to keep going. Not that there are not any struggles on the other road, because there will be, but on that right road Jesus will be walking with you. So walk with Jesus on that right road.

"Walk with Jesus on that Right Road"

Standing at the Crossroads
a few years ago.
I was torn between two signs,
Not knowing which was to go.

The sign on the left said,
come on grab all the gusto you can.
The sign on the right road,
seemed to keep pointing to one man.

The sign on the left said,
"Hurry up, life is passing you by."
The sign on the right road said,
"Choose this road and you will never die."

The sign on the left said,
"Come on join us in our so called fun and pleasure.
The sign on the right said,
Love, happiness, peace and a treasure.

The left road seemed
dark as night.
The right road,
was nothing but light.

The sign on the left said, Come on,
we do what we want, we're in control.
The sign on the right said,
walk with Jesus, he'll save your soul.

So I finally looked on the left road up ahead,
and seen a tiny little sign, it said, Dead End.
Then I looked on the right road up ahead,
and seen a sign that said, Come on let Jesus be your friend.

I'm sorry to say now,
I took the left road in my haste.
I got a little ways and woke up, I cried,
Lord forgive me my life is such a waste.

He said, "My Child,
just turn around and come back.
For with my promises
I am not slack."

That road has nothing to offer
but heartache and pain.
So walk with me on the right road,
and your life will not be in vain."

Jesus took my hand and helped me,
get back on the right road.
And Praise the Lord Jesus,
he took my heavy load!

Which road are you walking on? It is either one or the other. I am not saying are you walking perfect? But on one road we are walking without Jesus and the other road we are walking with Jesus on his highway.

"The King's Highway"

One day I was walking
down the road all alone.
I did not know my way,
but I seen a light that so brightly shone.

It wasn't just any light,
that I have ever seen before.
Oh! No! This light I saw before me,
it was, Oh! so much more.

This light was from a man,
at the end of my road.
This man he knew my name,
he knew my heavy load.

He said, Dear Friend, let me take you,
forever by the hand.
If you will love me and trust me,
I'll take you to your Promised Land.

So I did as he said,
and I gladly took his hand.
And from that day,
I've been walking with this man.

This man is so special,
He's the dearest friend I know.
He loves me so much, he lifts me up,
when I am feeling low.

I love him
more and more.
It's Jesus sweet Jesus,
He's the one that I adore.

He's warned me of some valleys
we would go through on our way.
But he's always reassured me,
I'd make it through, he would say.

Oftentimes while we were walking,
up this narrow road,
he would remind me, he was there,
to take my heavy load.

He would ask me to just praise him,

and be glad I was found.
He told me not to worry,
that he was always around.

He would gladly meet my needs,
whatever they were.
He keeps reminding me,
he loves me, I can be sure.

I'm here for everything you need,
please don't forget,
you have me, he tells me,
every need I have met.

Oftentimes I'm tempted to fear at the sights
along the way that could overwhelm my soul.
But then on my Jesus,
those cares, worries and fears I gladly roll.

Sometimes it seems impossible to go another step.
Then I watch this Jesus who has brought me through before.
He assures me and encourages me,
to go that one step more.

I am amazed at his glory.
Oh! How he has brought me through.
There is nothing, no nothing,
my Jesus cannot do.

Oftentimes I get cold and weary,
and feel the bitter winds blow.
Bitter winds of persecution on my soul.
But I'm on the King's Highway and to my King Jesus I go.

So when times I may not feel
Jesus by my side.
He reminds me,

in his arms I safely abide!

He just holds me and breathes on me
and reminds me and lets me know.
He is never, ever
gonna let me go.

Sometimes while we're walking along,
we come to a place with a lot of debris.
He says my child just stand,
and my salvation you will see.

He tells me to just stand
and wait and be still.
While he clears the way
and works his perfect will.

He's the one that really cares,
for he has died for me.
Only by his blood,
I am now set free.

Others may laugh and mock me
but it doesn't matter what they say.
For this one holding my hand is all
that is going to matter come judgment day.
Sometimes as we walk
along, others may try,
to take what I have with this friend of mine.
But he just defends me,
and makes them get in line.

They just don't know
when I gave him my heart,
he promised me,
that we would never part.
in me he'd finish what he did start.

They don't understand when they mock me
that this man, Jesus is God's only Son!
And I put my faith in him,
he and I are one.

The victory is mine, It is finished
they can't take it from me what Jesus has done.
So if they don't accept him,
they better leave me alone!

Sometimes along this road when it seems
I'll never get out of this valley.
I'll look at him and question
"How long is it going to be?"

For it seems like we'll never
get to the other side.
He tells me to trust him,
that this valley is not really that wide.

He says this valley is not
really that long either compared to eternity.
He tells me this valley is a blessing,
and one day soon I shall see!

He says my child since you've been in this valley,
you've learned to lean on me and depend.
So see this valley has strengthened, never harmed,
only caused you to trust me as your friend.

And on this road Jesus tells me,
never to grumble and gripe.
For my life is hid in him now,
and my tear's he doth wipe.

And often when tempted
to grumble and complain,

he reminds me I'm passing through,
and I have Heaven to Gain.

My Jesus often tells me, "Rejoice,
For my sins are washed away."
Then I remember who I am walking with,
on "The King's Highway!"

What an awesome thought! We don't have to walk this life alone! God paid a tremendous price for us, so we could fellowship with him. So we would not ever have to be lonely again. He sent Jesus his only begotten Son, to die for you, so you don't ever have to be lonely! Doesn't that make life worth living? This world down here can be such a lonely place. And sometimes we don't get the love and affection we expect from people. Maybe a husband or wife, or other loved ones do not pay us the attention our hearts so desperately long for. And sometimes it may appear that no one really loves us. Well! It may appear to be like that, but God loves us. He sent Jesus so we could be adopted in his family. And he would be our Father. When we ask Jesus to forgive us for our sins, we become God's child. God becomes our Heavenly Father! Never, ever to be lonely again. For only Jesus can fill that longing in our heart for love. It was put there by God, for Jesus to fill. No-one else can fill it. Our Father God takes such excellent care of his children. When we come to him through Jesus, he accepts us, and loves us, and holds us and we will never, ever be lonely again. No trial can ever separate us from his love. Nothing or no-one can snatch you out of his hands. We have his love and life, what more could we want? So no matter what you are going through right now, and no matter how lonely it appears you are. Right now, thank God for sending Jesus to die for you. Your sins personally! And right now thank him for making you his child, and for never leaving you, never forsaking you, and for always holding you.

"Unseen Hands are Holding You!"

You may not have had,
a daddy to hold you,
along this pilgrim way.
Remember there is unseen hands,
holding and guiding you,
even in your darkest day.

If you believe in Jesus,
you have a Heavenly Father,
who is watching his children to protect.
And the slightest bit of harm,
to his children, he will detect.

He will not let anything harm us,
not even the trials
a child of God goes through.
For even in them
he'll turn the bad around for our good too.

Sometimes along this way, we may crave,
for others' affection.
Often they turn us away,
and we only get rejection.

They may be cruel
and sometimes treat us wrong,
for our love in return.
But there is one thing, even through that,
that Jesus wants us to learn.

The times you may feel
persecuted and mocked,
all alone and forsaken.
Jesus knows exactly how you feel
those very step's he has taken.

He knows how it feels to be rejected,
persecuted and despised.
And if that happens while serving him,
you should not be surprised.

As it says in God's Word
the servant is not greater than the master.
If we can remember this very truth,
we'll grow in these trials a whole lot faster.

They persecuted our Lord
and rejected him even to his death.
But death was swallowed up in victory.
So no matter the trials
they are one day, going to end in Glory.

So when things are happening
that we question, and can't understand.
Rest assured, our Heavenly Father loves us,
and he does have a plan.

A plan to always strengthen and help us.
Never, ever can we be harmed.
So be Faithful, be sober.
Our Heavenly Father holds us,
so lets not be alarmed!

Father God is holding you! Just rest in his arms. He loves you and no-one or anything can ever snatch you out of his hands. Jesus says in John 10:28, "And I give unto them eternal life; and they shall never perish, neither shall any man pluck them out of my hand. v. 29. My Father, which gave them me, is greater than all, and no man is able to pluck them out of my Father's hand. v. 30. I and my Father are one." No one is able to pluck you out of the Father's hand. No trial, no sorrow, no persecution, no war, no nothing can separate you. God says in Romans 8:35, "Who shall separate us from the love of Christ? Shall trouble, or distress, or persecution, or famine, or nakedness, or peril, or war. Then in v. 37, He says, "Nay, in all these things we are more than conquerors, through him that loved us. v. 38. For I am persuaded that neither death, nor life, nor angels, nor principalities, nor powers, nor things present, nor things to come, v. 39. Nor height, nor depth, nor any other creature, shall be able to separate us from the Love of God, which is in Christ Jesus our Lord." Whatever it is you are going through right now please remember Jesus Loves You! And nothing can separate you from his love.

I am in awe of God's Love and Mercy. I am so thankful that his love never dies. He doesn't just love you when you are good. He loves you always! Unconditionally! He doesn't just love you just when you think you've been good and deserve it. No! He loves you also when you feel like a failure and unlovable.

"Unmeasureless Love"

Oh! For the Love
that never dies.
Bringing Comfort
to my tear-filled, eyes.

Living water springing up,
within my soul.
Giving joy and life,
making me whole.

Comforting Love,
no words express.
No failure of mine,
to make it less.

No trouble, nor trial
to make depart,
the Love of God,

from my Heart.

No heartache or pain
to make it fail.
Over death or sorrow,
it doth Prevail!

You know some times this life on earth brings so much pain and so much sorrow. And sometimes we may even question God's love. The Pain is so great! And we may think God, if you love me why are you letting this happen or why did you let this happen to me. Where is your Love? You know there really are no easy answers. We can't always explain every little detail of our lives. And sometimes we have so many questions. But I can tell you this much, God loves you and he is there! He is the Answer! Jesus is the Answer! He is the only one that can take away that pain. Maybe you have lost a loved one through death and right now you are filled with so much sorrow. You have so many questions. You may be confused. You had so many plans. And you might even feel hurt and angry that death has come and you feel so lost and empty, with no hope and no direction now. You may have even thought what is the use for me going on anymore. And the pain and sorrow may be just too much for you to bear. Jesus knows, and he carried that sorrow for you. When Jesus walked that road to Golgotha carrying that cross, that weighed so heavy on him, it was for you! All of your sorrows, all of your grief, were what that cross represents for you!

"There will Always be a Place"

Life is filled
with troubles and trials.
Wanting acceptance,
with no denials.

No rejections
do we want.

Only everyone
our confidante.

But reality hits,
and then we find.
Not everyone
pays us a mind.

Not everyone
gives us their time.
And very soon, you may say,
life is not always peace sublime.

Heartaches may stay
more than people you know.
You find yourself
with no where to go.

Just remember when
hopeless and lost.
That Jesus paid for you,
a priceless cost.

He died on the cross
for you, your soul.
Oh! How he wants
to make you whole.

He loves you more,
than you can ever imagine.
No matter what you've done,
or where you have been.

Just look to Jesus,
find life anew,
for at the cross,
there is always a place for you!

In Isaiah 53:3, Isaiah is prophesying about our Lord Jesus Christ. He is despised and rejected, a man of sorrows and acquainted with grief, and we hid as it were our faces from him; he was despised and we appreciated him not. Surely he hath borne our griefs and carried our sorrow's; yet we did esteem him stricken, smitten of God, and afflicted. But he was wounded for our transgressions, he was bruised for our iniquities; the chastisement of our peace was upon him; and with his stripes we are healed." Jesus knows your sorrows! He knows your griefs. Nobody on the face of this earth may understand what you are going through. But let me tell you, Jesus knows! He bore that very grief you have right now. He carried those sorrows that you are carrying. So you don't have to carry them any longer.

"I Did This For You!"

I did this for you,
my child, please listen to my story.
I came down
from my portals in glory.

From my ivory palaces
and streets of gold.in Heaven,
to a world full of care, full of sin.
To be born by a virgin,
named, "Mary".
So Pure and so Fair, without, within.

I was born in a manger
so long ago.
I walked this earth, in the flesh.
So pain and heartache I know!

All the way to Calvary
I was beaten and bruised,
I was despised, rejected,
hurt and abused.

I bore the sorrow,
suffering and shame.
I took your place, my child,
So when you would call on my name,
everything you need, in your life,
you can boldly claim.

For I did this all for you.
So believe on me,
and your life I will renew!

Yes, Dear Lord,
all the stripes, hurt and pain,
on the cross you bore.
Lord, I appreciate it. It was not in vain,
Oh! Lord your cross I won't ignore.

Jesus bore your griefs. He carried your sorrows. So you don't have to. Wherever you are at right now, give him your pain and heartache. In Psalms 34:18, "David says, "The Lord is near unto them that are of a broken heart and saveth such as be of a crushed spirit." If you are hurting and your heart is breaking, Jesus Christ is right there beside you. Whether you feel him or not. By faith he is there. Just like you can't see the wind, but it is there and you can see the affects of it. God is there!

•

"God is There!"

So many times I've cried out,
to God in deep despair.
I sometimes even wondered,
if he was really there.

I said impatiently how long
does this pain have to go on?
Jesus then reminds me,

when I am weak, he is strong.

Though the storms are raging
high around you.
Just trust in me,
cause I feel the things you do.

Every hurt you've had,
every tear you've shed.
It was for you, too,
that I died and bled.

But I arose the third day,
and am no longer dead.
And he says my child, I know,
the very numbers of hairs on your head.

Please don't doubt
but only believe.
And all the things
I've promised, you will receive.

God says in Romans 10:9, "That if thou shalt confess with thy mouth the Lord Jesus Christ, and shalt believe with thine heart that God raised him from the dead, thou shalt be saved. v. 10. For with the heart man believeth unto righteousness and with the mouth confession is made unto salvation. v. 11. For the scripture saith, whosoever believeth in him shall not be ashamed. v. 12. For there is no difference between the Jew and the Greek; For the same Lord over all is rich unto all that call upon him. v. 13. For whosoever shall call upon the name of the Lord shall be saved." Sometimes when we are hurting we may have a hard time believing that God loves us. And we may struggle with our doubts which only compound our problems. But there is Hope if we can only believe! Believe that Jesus is there for you. He is right there next to you. Talk to him and let him heal whatever is troubling you. There was a man a long time ago whose son was demon possessed and it was causing him and his son much pain. He wanted so bad for his Son to be delivered and set free. The man went to the only one who could heal him. Jesus Christ! No, he did not go to any psychologist, doctor, or television talk show. He went to the only one that truly loved him. Now, don't get me wrong, I am definitely not against going to doctors or counselors. By all means if your child is sick and needing help get that baby to a doctor! But don't exclude Jesus either. Pray to Jesus first. I mean why go to Jesus as a last resort? Getting back to that story about that boy. And Jesus asked him, How long is it Since this came unto him? And the man said, When he was a child." That man was probably filled with so much torment and sorrow. Having to watch his son all of those years to almost be destroyed. God says in Mark 9:22, "And many times it would cast him into the fire, and into the waters to destroy him." Oh! The pain and torment that boy must have been through. And the heartache that father must have been carrying. Watching that happen to his son many times. Maybe you have a son or daughter or loved one that may be on drugs or alcohol. Or you might have a loved one in jail. Or maybe you have a loved one that is easily angered and it is absolutely breaking your heart. Go to the only one who can deliver, set free and heal. Go to Jesus. For like he told that man in Mark 9:23, "If thou can believe, all things are possible to him that believeth." Maybe you are saying, Oh! I would like to believe that but I don't know if I can. You may have almost given up all hope. And you may be saying, Oh! I want to believe, and I try to, but I've been through so much! Jesus will help your unbelief. Don't be scared to be honest with Jesus. He loves you. You can talk to him. That man received a miracle, when he was honest with Jesus. Jesus said to him, If thou canst believe all things are possible to him, that believeth. The Word of God says in Mark 9:24, "And immediately the Father of the child cried out, and said with tears, Lord, I believe, help thou mine unbelief. And Jesus did just that. You can just hear the desperation in that Father's heart, when he cried. He was really saying, if my child's deliverance is hanging in the balance over whether I believe or not. Oh! My Lord please help me! He was scared that if he did not believe enough it was all over for his son and him. Because he probably could not take it anymore. Jesus seen that man's broken heart.

So he healed him. I've heard people say that it is not your need that Jesus sees and acts upon, but it is your faith. It does move Jesus when he sees even your broken heart. He is not waiting on you to become like "Smith Wigglesworth" who was a great man of faith. Only come to him like you are and be honest with him. He wants a relationship with you. He wants to heal your broken heart.

"He is the Healer of your Broken Heart"

You may be hurting
and in much pain,
and may be all broken hearted.
You may be sorrowful and feeling hopeless,
over dreams and plans
and joy's all departed.

You may think you don't have
anyone you can love,
or anyone to trust.
You know you can't go on,
living like you are,
for sooner or later, to love and trust, you must.

For we were created not to be alone,
but to love and be loved,
while living here below.
For love gives us life,
and makes it worth living,
and love surely makes us grow.

So let the walls fall down
and give it all to Jesus,
let him in today.
He cares for you.
All the hurt and all the pain,
just give it all to him when you pray.

For he is love and him you can trust.
He's the Healer today,
of your broken heart.
Let it all go, forget the past,
he'll wash you clean,
and give you a new start.

Let him come in and heal your broken heart. Jesus says in Revelation 3:20, "Behold, I stand at the door and knock, if any man hear my voice, and open the door, I will come in to him, and will sup with him and he with me." When you are hurting, give it to Jesus. You can trust him to take over.

"Just Leave it to Jesus"

Just Leave it to Jesus,
to change your life.
Just take it to him,
every hurt, pain and strife.

Just Leave it to Jesus,
When times are hard
Don't get discouraged,
and your dreams discard.

Just leave it to Jesus,
to come and restore.
He'll come and shield you,
He'll be around you, behind you, in you and before.

Just leave it to Jesus
to walk you through the trials.
Just leave it to Jesus,
to go the extra miles.

Just leave it to Jesus,

to lift you when you are low.
When all of your friends have left you,
he'll be there, that I know.

Just leave it to Jesus to come,
when you think you can't go another step.
He gives power to the faint.
He gives you zeal, life and pep.

Just leave it to Jesus,
to show up when you need him.
To come with healing in his hands.
Just leave it to Jesus, to be your strength,
during all of life's demands.

Just leave it to Jesus to show up,
when you think there is absolutely no hope.
Just leave it to him, to take over,
when you think you just cannot cope.

Just leave it to Jesus to say,
Hey! Cheer up, weeping won't last.
Just leave it to him to wipe all the tears,
to give you joy, and erase all the past.

Just leave it to Jesus to come in the nick of time.
Satan whispers, "It's all over, you might as well quit."
Just leave it to Jesus to tell him,
to go back to the pit.

Just leave it to Jesus to come, after you've prayed
and it seems things are getting worse.
When Satan whispers, tempts and taunts.
And in your mind, his doubts he doth rehearse.

When Satan whispers, see, for you it won't work,
this so-called "Faith" walk.

He tries to make you doubt, fear and disbelieve.
That's what he wants you to talk.

But just leave it to Jesus to take control,
and turn things around.
Leave it to him to help you,
keep the faith to pick you off of the ground.

Just leave it to Jesus to turn
even the things Satan is putting you through.
Just leave it to Jesus to turn even them
around for your good, too.

When Satan will whisper
you will never make it home.
Leave it to Jesus to say, this one has been broken,
on me he depends, he will never roam.

Just leave it to Jesus to look at Satan and say,
though you desire to sift this one as wheat,
And though old Satan,
you put this one through the heat.

Just leave it to Jesus to tell Satan he will make it,
for I'm praying for him, his faith will not fail.
Just leave it to Jesus to throw Satan one day soon,
in that pit called Hell!

Too many times when we are going through struggles, heartaches and especially disappointments with others, we do not leave it to Jesus to help us. We take matters into our own hands. And when we do that we are in trouble. Sometimes we stay burdened down and worried, over things we have no control. We refuse to let go of our control to Jesus. When things are out of control, we refuse to confess the problems we are having. We try to put on a happy face and say I'm alright, I'm cool, everything is okay. We try to have a tight grip on our lives not wanting to admit we are out of control. Sometimes through tradition we are taught to just handle things. We are taught to pull ourselves up by our bootstraps and tough things out. The thing with that is we can't do that. Not on our own. We need a Savior! We all do. In Romans 3:23 Paul says, "For all have sinned and come short of the glory of God." Every one of us needs a Savior. There is hope for our lives when we recognize we need Jesus! When we realize we cannot save ourselves. We may try to save ourselves by trying to be good. We may go to church and get our name on a membership roll. But that is not going to save us. Only when we realize how utterly hopeless we are, and we are not in control, can we then find hope in Jesus. God says, "He that covereth his sins shall not prosper, but he that confesseth and forsaketh them shall have mercy." And then in James 2:13 James says, "Mercy is a joy against judgment." If we try to cover our sins, we will not have mercy. But judgment is what we have. It does not matter how good we think we are, or have been. We cannot save ourselves. Only by the blood of Jesus, are we saved. Only by the blood of Jesus there is hope.

"It's in the Blood!"

You may think
you are a good person,
you try to do your best.
Well, stop trying, trust in Jesus,
and you will be truly blest.
For life is in his blood,
so come to him all who are weary,
and he shall give you rest.

All you who are heavy laden
and burdened down with care.
Let it go, give it to Jesus, for life is in his blood,
he will help all your troubles bear.

It's not by just joining a church,

or going through, some religious routine.
But life is in the blood of Jesus
and a relationship with him
and on him you must lean.

It's not just by getting your name
on a membership roll.
But life is in the blood of Jesus,
For only his blood, can cleanse your soul.

Life is in the blood of Jesus
He can make you whole.
For only Jesus, with his blood,
can write your name in the Lamb's Book of Life,
on his, "Heavenly Roll."

You cannot and will not have life or hope apart from Jesus. If you want life, if you want hope call on Jesus. He will hear your faintest cry.

"If"

If you are lonely - Jesus is There!
If you are hurting - Jesus does care!
If you can't cope - Jesus is Hope!
If you need Love - Jesus share's from above.
If you need wisdom - Jesus Teaches!
If you are in a hole - Jesus Reaches!
If you can't go another step - Jesus Carries!
If you're Bound - Jesus Frees!
If you feel forsaken - Jesus never leaves!

If you are feeling like no-one loves you, no-one at all understands you and if you are feeling rejected, hurt and abused, Jesus knows how you feel. He walked this earth in the flesh. I remember a time I was deeply hurt by someone whom I really, really loved. And as I got in my car and was driving home, I just started telling my Lord how I felt. I was hurt and angry at the same time. So I just started spilling everything out to my Lord. Then all of a sudden I started remembering what all Jesus had gone through. And then I heard my Lord say, "I know. I know exactly how you feel".

"I Know How it Feels"

One day while traveling along
an old country road.
I was feeling very angry,
under the heavy load.

It seemed like people
get away with doing you wrong.
And it seems at times,
the nights last so very, very long.

I discussed with my Lord Jesus
just how I was feeling.
It felt so good to tell Jesus
my innermost thoughts, my innermost feelings.
For my heart was hurting,
and it really needed a healing.

I said, "Lord, this really hurts."
Then he says, "I know how it feels."
Just knowing Jesus was with me,
his presence and smile really heals.

There may be times when no one at all understands you. And sometimes you may not necessarily care if anyone else has the answers. Sometimes you may want someone just to be there. Sometimes it just helps to know you are not alone. You know you may be sitting there right now and it appears you are all by yourself. But really you are not alone! Jesus is there and he loves you and he knows what you are going through. He knows what you are facing. He knows that court date that you have tomorrow. He knows the load you bear. And only knowing he is with you, you can make it!

"It Helps to Know!"

It helps to know
when I'm going through,
the valley so dark, nothing I can see.
My precious Lord,
never takes his eyes off of me.
It helps to know, he is seeing for me.

When the way is long
and I can't go another step,
from carrying such a heavy load.
It helps to know,
you are there when I am traveling all alone,
down a rough and rocky road.

When things along the way
that I don't understand, and make my heart break.
It helps to know, you Lord, are with me,
and me you will never forsake.

When walking through the fire,
with hot coals under my feet.
When the enemy tries to destroy me,
by turning up the heat.
It helps to know, Lord, you carry me,
and keep me, so I won't know defeat.

It helps to know
when the enemy comes and tells me,
"My Lord won't forgive me any longer.
You tell me Lord, "I'm going to have trials.
They're not to finish me, but to only make me stronger."

When the enemy whispers, "It's Over!
And tells me it's the end."
It moves me closer to you,
I run to you and depend.
It helps to know Lord, you love me,
and you are my dearest friend.

The only thing in this world that matters, is knowing Jesus! Knowing that he is with you when you are going through the most horrific circumstances. Maybe financial trouble, family trouble, or a death of a loved one it helps to know he is with you! You can have all the head knowledge there is in this world. You might be a very intelligent person but it does not matter without Jesus! I am not saying that God does not expect us to use our brains. Because he does expect us to use what he has given us. But no amount of head knowledge can save your soul, and give you hope, life and peace. If we have Jesus, he is all we need!

All We Need!

For his Word is sufficient to guide me, on my way.
When the storms arise and try to drown my soul.

All I need is to know,
my cares, on him I can roll.

Because of Jesus
I have hope for today.
All I need, is to know
he hears me when I pray.

All I need to be happy is to know,
I'm on the road.
Leading straight to Heaven
to my Heavenly abode.

Walking with my Jesus,
who is taking care of me.
So to keep me Happy,
that's enough
For me!

We all have to come to the point that we all need Jesus to keep us happy. We can search this whole world over for happiness. We can climb the "corporate ladder", so to speak. And strive to make more and more money. But it still is not going to be enough to fill that emptiness in your heart. You can even be doing good deeds to try to make yourself feel happy or worth something. But it will not take away that hole you have in your heart. That was put there by Father God for Jesus to fill. Only Jesus can satisfy your soul. No amount of money, no amount of fame. No amount of popularity can take away that loneliness in your heart. And until we get to that point, where you don't want anything else other than Jesus, we will live a hopeless, miserable life. If you are feeling hopeless, call on Jesus. Nothing in this world will satisfy your heart. Drugs cannot satisfy, alcohol cannot satisfy. Only Jesus can take that loneliness out of your heart.

"Search No More!"

There is no more reason to live
in the degradation of sin.
No more reason
to dread another day to begin.

No more reason, to be all,
down and out.
No more reason
to live in pity and pout.

No more reason
to search the world over,
to fill that emptiness in your heart.
No more reason
to leave your family,
to have a new start.

No more reason to drink,
your problems away.
For the search is over,
for you today.

I'm right here beside you.
And I am the Lord.
If you let me into your heart,
and take heed to my word.

I'll fill that emptiness,
in your heart.
I'll never forsake you,
No we'll never part.

So search no farther.Don't you know,

you've really been looking for me.
Search no more.
I'm here to set you free!

You may have went from relationship to relationship, and still are not satisfied. That is the way God created you. Only he can make you complete.

"Only Jesus Satisfies!"

Jesus satisfied my hungry, longing soul.
He touched my hollow heart,
and forever made me whole.
He filled me with his Holy Spirit,
and my life he does control.

I no longer want the things of this world
to try to satisfy.
Just knowing I will be
forever with Jesus, in the sweet by and by.
Is enough to make me sing, shout,
dance and make me high.

So if you're down and defeated
and longing for some kind of fix,
Well, Jesus and the world don't mix.

Get rid of worldly things, give Jesus a try.
And your heart he will surely satisfy!

Jesus says in Matthew 5, "Blessed are ye that hunger and thirst after righteousness, for they shall be filled." What do ye hunger and thirst for? What makes you keep going? Is it money, material things? Do you live everyday to make more money because you want a fancy car, or a bigger house. Or maybe you live just to please your spouse or family. Maybe you say, if I could just be with that person, I would be so happy. If I could just be married to him, my life would be better. Then you may finally get that one that you desperately went after, and you are still not happy. Because you have to walk on egg shells to keep them. And now you find yourself more unhappy than ever. You soon find out, that that one was not what you wanted or needed at all. All that has happened was you compounded your unhappiness, loneliness and despair. And it has left you feeling hopeless and depressed. I'd like to tell you that the search is over. Jesus loves you! He is the only one you need. No-one on the face of this earth can love you like Jesus. He died for you. Call on him and commit to him and he will take you and love you more than you could ever imagine. Let him be the love of your life.

"Searching for Someone?"

Everyone wants someone
whom they can call their own.
There are so many hurting people.
So many are alone.

I know one who will love you,
to me, his love he has shone.
He's proven to be faithful,
to everyone he has known.

His name is Jesus
God's Son.
Call on him today,
and your life has just begun.

He's everything you've longed for
and oh! so much more.
He will never leave you,
you can trust him to be sure.

Everyone wants someone
when nights can be so long.
When days are short,
and you don't know how to carry on.

I know one who will hold you
and never let you go.
This someone is so special,
he is so good to know.

Just take a look at Calvary
and your love for him will grow.
For no-one has ever died for you,
look how he loves you so.

Everyone wants someone
on whom to take a chance.
Someone to share their life
through every circumstance.

That someone is Jesus,
he will be there for you.
Just talk to him, he loves you,
no matter what you do.

Just pour your heart out to him,
he's a true friend you will find.
There's no other one just like him.
Who is faithful, true and kind.

So let him now come in,
and the search will be over today.

Forget about everything else,
talk to him and pray.

The call is free,
you won't even need a dime.
Jesus has been waiting
for you all this time.

So now the search is over,
search no more.
For Jesus is there,
right at your hearts door.

There was a time in my life before I met Jesus that the emptiness was so deep in my heart. And because of that I just did not want to go on any longer. I went from relationship to relationship trying to make it go away. Drinking would not fill it. Staying busy would not take it away. Had Jesus not met me or shall I say had I not met Jesus when I did I would probably be in Hell right now or in a mental ward somewhere wanting to die. I could not take the loneliness and pain any longer. Jesus is the only one that picked me up and loved me like I needed to be loved. I am not saying that I didn't have friends and that my parents didn't love me because they all did. But even they misunderstood me. Even they could not figure out why I was so unhappy and acted the way I did because of it. Even they grew impatient with me and didn't have the time for me that I needed. Even they grew weary of me and my problems. But there was one that always understood me. He always had time and never turned me away. And that was Jesus.

"You're the one Lord Jesus"

Sometimes when I feel all alone
and need a friend just to care.
When everyone else doesn't understand
Jesus you are always there.

When everyone else doesn't have time,
and often turns me away.
Jesus you are always there
all the night and all of the day.

When sometimes it's hard to say what I feel
and let my feelings out.
All I have to do is talk to you Jesus.
For you know me, what I am all about.

You know my every weakness
and you know my every care.
And with all of my trials
without you Lord, I could never bear.

It's always been you Lord
to lift me up when I felt low.
You'd help me realize
hard times are what makes me grow.

Sometimes even our own spouse does not understand us. But Jesus does. He knows why we do and say the things we do out of our own pain. Sometimes we may hurt others because we are hurt ourselves. Jesus understands and he wants to help us to be complete in him. So many times we cling to others or things to make us feel whole and complete. Jesus does say to leave father and mother and cleave to your wife. However, he does not say to put them before Jesus. We get so dependent on others to take away that longing in our hearts. And no one can take it away except for Jesus. Paul says in Colossians 2:6, "As ye have therefore received Jesus Christ our Lord, so walk ye in him, v. 7 "Rooted and built up in him and established in the faith, as ye have been taught, abounding therein with thanksgiving. v. 8. Beware lest any man spoil you through philosophy and vain deceit, after the tradition of men, after the principles of the world and not after Christ. v. 9. For in him dwelleth all the fullness of the Godhead bodily. v. 10. And ye are complete in him, which is the head of all rule and power." If you have received Jesus Christ as your Lord, walk in him, be rooted and built up in him, and established in the faith, follow Him. Don't follow the world. Don't follow what anyone tells you. Follow Jesus, who is the head of all rule and authority. Remember if you have Jesus you are complete in him. You don't have to go from relationship to relationship seeking happiness. You don't have to have anyone try to convince you that man has evolved, and that creation isn't real. You don't have to have anyone's opinion on anything. When you meet Jesus, all the questions in your mind will be solved. For you will know where to go with them. Jesus is the only answer you need. You don't need philosophy, psychology or even religion. 1 John 2:20 says, "But ye have an anointing from the Holy One, and ye know all things, v. 26 says, "These things have I written unto you concerning them that deceive you, but the anointing which ye have received of him abideth in you, and ye need not that any man teach you; but as the same anointing teacheth you of all things, and is truth, and is no lie, and even as it hath taught you, ye shall abide in him. " Many people run to and fro seeking truth, seeking answers. And are left feeling tired, frustrated and more and more confused. It is like they are in a desert and they are struggling and are weary from trying everything there is to try to quench their hungry, thirsty souls. There is a well in our desert. Amidst all of the heat, all of the deadness and all of the dryness.

"A Well in the Desert"

Once I felt like I was in a desert,
all alone, thirsty and dry.
I struggled and struggled
as I watched the day go by.

I'd fall down on my face,
because I could not go on anymore.
I'd get back up and go again,
then I'd fall as I did before.

I cried out to the Lord
and asked him to make the rain pour.
He told me to get up
and go again once more.

He told me to get up and turn around,
then keep going straight ahead.
He told me he wasn't going to leave me here,
in this desert for dead.

So I did as he told me
and I took him at his word.
Then Praise the Lord
the Rain had poured!

For Jesus says, "If any man thirst,
Let him come unto me and drink.
So if you are in a desert
to this water, Jesus is your only link.

So now no more struggling
and no more strife.
For Jesus is truly
"The Wellspring of Life."

There was a lady whom Jesus went to her town, (the town of Samaria). He went there especially for her that day. He had an appointment with her although she did not know it. This lady had been broken I'm sure and had a lot of heartache. For she had been married five times, and the man she was living with now was not her husband. Jesus knew that, yet he loved her anyway. He did not condemn her like people would. He didn't stay away from her so she would not "influence him". No. He loved her and wanted her to receive his love that day. He knew she needed him. He knew of her pain and heartache. And how she was feeling so broken and torn apart from all of the broken relationships she had from her past. Jesus went to make her whole. In

John 4 Jesus was wearied from his Journey and he sat down by Jacob's well, and the Lady came to draw water from the well. Jesus knew she was going to come there that day. Just like he knows you are reading this book right now.

"He Knows All About You"

If sometimes the road
is rocky and rough.
And you think you've had
just about enough.

Just remember you have
a friend.
Who is right there beside you.
He's one on whom you can depend.

You may think
no one understands.
But Just talk to Jesus
for your life is in his hands.

He knows your frame
and he knows we are but dust.
So if the road is long and hard,
on Jesus put your trust.

He knows your heartache. He knows how people have misunderstood you. He knows how you have been hollered at, and abused and thrown away like something worthless. He, however, sees you as very valuable! Enough to die for.

"Everything and Everyone is Valuable"

Oh! Father, I marvel
at your creation.
At the trees, the mountains,
the grass and the ocean.

Everything is perfect and lovely
in your eyes.
We know you've created this world.
We don't have to surmise.

Everything is created for your glory.
The seas, the heavens, every creature on earth.
Every single thing, you have created.
Every single thing has worth!

Everything and everyone is valuable.
On this you are reliable, you have not made one mistake.
You are a wonderful Father,
and everything is special you make!

Jesus sees you as very valuable. He died for you. If you were the only one on the face of this earth he would have came and died for you. In John 4:7 Jesus asked the Samaritan woman to give him a drink and in v. 9 she says to Jesus, "How is it that thou a Jew askest drink of me, which am a woman of Samaria? For the Jews have no dealings with the Samaritans." She was feeling so unworthy to even talk to Jesus because of tradition. Because other people made her feel so looked down upon and so unworthy. Jesus is so loving and kind, he does not look down upon anyone. Jesus says in John 6:37, "All that the Father giveth me shall come to me; and him that cometh to me I will in no wise cast out." You have his word right there. He that cometh to him he will in no wise cast out! No way, no how will he cast you out when you come to him. No matter what you have done. Jesus told the Samaritan woman in John 4:10, "If thou knewest the gift of God, and who it is that saith to thee, Give me to drink; thou would have asked of him, and he would have given thee living water." Jesus is saying, If you only knew what he has in store for you! Don't let the fear of rejection or the spirit of rejection stop you from knowing Jesus and his love. Receive his love for he loves you so much! The Samaritan woman in v. 11 could not figure out with her natural mind, how he was going to give her water out of that well for he had nothing to draw it out with. But Jesus was not talking about other wells that you could see, feel or touch with your natural hands or sight. Oh! He was talking about a well that comes straight from the throne of God. One that you can drink from anytime of the day or night. A well that is "Happy Hour" every second of the day or night. A well that is a continual supply. That never, ever runs dry. Jesus tells the woman in John 4:13, (talking about Jacobs well), "Whosoever drinketh of this water shall thirst again." Jesus says in v. 14 "But whosoever drinketh of the water that I shall give him shall never thirst, but the water that I shall give him shall be in him a well of water springing up into everlasting life." It is by faith we can drink from this well. Do you wake in. the morning and hate to see another day begin? I'm not talking about just having a bad day. Because we all have them sometimes. But do you feel like you have no purpose, no meaning or no direction? You just feel like you are trying to survive in a cold, cruel world. And you really don't know why. You grumble and complain saying, "Well, I didn't ask to be here, it was my Dad and Mom's fault I am here!" No, it is God's fault. He put you here for a reason. Now doesn't that make you feel special? He created you to love and worship him. And only when you start doing that will you be truly happy. That emptiness, that hunger and thirst you have right now is put there by God. And you are really hungering and thirsting for Jesus. You may not know it but you are. You may have listened to other people try to explain to you the meaning of life. You may hear them say, Oh! laying around the beach is the life. You have heard them say, having money, fame and popularity is the way of life. You may have listened to the worlds' greatest philosophers, but if they have not led you to Jesus, it has left you more and more confused. For Jesus is the Way, the Truth and the Life. Or you may have heard of Jesus and you may think, "Yes,

He is a great teacher." Well, he is more than just a great teacher. He is the only teacher you need. He is more than a teacher. He is God! He is the only God there is!

"Only One God!"

Twinkle, Twinkle I wish I might I wish I may.
I heard you so boldly, so childlike say.
Well I have to tell you, there's only one life
one truth, one way!
And that's to the God who made those stars,
to whom we should pray.
Only one God, Only one God,
Only one God today.
Only one God, Only one God,
who is not far away!
He's just as close
as the mention of his name you say.
in the name of Jesus
he'll hear you when you pray.

So there's only one God,
to depend upon.
One star to wish upon.
The star on the cross of Calvary,
Jesus God's Son.

So look to him and put your trust.
For he's a real wish come true.
It's about more than a wish upon a star.
For Jesus really died for you!

And there's no God that answers like our God.
For our God answers by Fire.
For all that call on him.

even out of the muck and mire.

For he never turns a deaf ear to us.
He hears our faintest cry.
For he alone, is God Almighty,
all other so-called gods he will defy.
So worship Him and on him only rely!

Turn from other gods, for He alone is worthy.
Let your All on the altar be laid.
He alone, your salvation,
he has paid.

So give Jesus today a call,
and his power you will see.
He will answer by fire.
And deliver, and set you free!

You may have heard of the name of Jesus, but now he has to get into your heart. It is more than just hearing. He wants us to love him with all of our heart. The woman at the well in the book of John said, "Sir, I perceive that thou art a Prophet. Our fathers worshipped in this Mountain; and ye say, that in Jerusalem is the place where men ought to worship, in verse 21, Jesus says, "Woman believe me, the hour cometh, when ye shall neither in this mountain, nor yet at Jerusalem, worship the Father. Ye worship ye know not what, we know what we worship; For salvation is of the Jews. v. 23. But the hour cometh and now is, when the true worshippers shall worship the Father in Spirit and in Truth; For the Father seeketh such to worship him. v. 24. God is a Spirit, and they that worship him must worship him in Spirit and in truth." God does not want us being concerned where we worship. He does not want us just being religious. He wants us to have a relationship with him. Jesus says when we drink of the water that comes from his well we shall never thirst again. But when we drink from the "wells" of this world, we shall thirst again. The so-called wells of this world cannot satisfy. I have heard people searching for the "Fountain of Youth". They try everything they can to hang on to life. But is that what they are really hanging on to? No, they are hanging on to death and false hope. When we believe in Jesus we find the fountain of youth. It is then that we have eternal life. Jesus says in John 11:25, "I am the Resurrection and the Life, he that believeth in me, though he were dead, yet shall he live; And whosoever liveth and believeth in me shall never die. Believest thou this?" When we know Jesus we don't have to worry about getting old or dying. When we know Jesus and believe in him to be who he says he is, the Resurrection and the Life, we will never die. We have eternal life! You may have heard of Jesus like that Samaritan woman in John 4:25, who said to Jesus, "I know that Messiah cometh which is called Christ, when he is come, he will tell us all things." See she had heard about Jesus, that he was the Messiah. She heard he was coming but until that day, she never met him and knew him with her heart. In verse 26 Jesus saith unto her, "I that speak unto thee am He." Then she knew God the Father revealed to her who Jesus was. His only begotten Son whom he sent into the world to die for our sins. No other God can touch your heart like Jesus and transform your life from the inside out. There may be other so-called "gods". But there is only one God alone. Some worship other gods like Buddha. But Buddha is dead. And Buddha can't answer! There is even no comparison! God is God alone! Jesus is the only one that can change a heart. Only he can take a hardened criminal and make him loving, kind and gentle. Only he can take a man or woman in adultery and make them repent and love him first.. But until he is in your heart and not just in your head, will you have joy. Many people have a bible in their house, and they may say, "Yes, I believe in God." And they may have pictures of Jesus on their walls, but until you "Take him off the Wall" and let him into your heart you will not experience the joy that only comes from knowing him with your whole being.

"Take Him off the Wall"

Take Him off of the Wall
and put him into your heart.
For we all need
his special Grace to us impart.

For He's more
than just a person hanging on a cross.
For living in this world of sin
will sometimes bring us loss.

He's more than just a person
hanging upon a wall.
He's our Lord and Savior,
to whosoever on him will call.

You have to know him personally
So give him your life today.
For he has to be more than a picture.
To Heaven, He is our only way!

Only you know in your own heart whether you have met Jesus and have a personal relationship with him or not. And when you meet Jesus no one can take him away from you or snatch you out of his hands. And no one can tell you when or where to worship him. And nobody can tell you to be quiet. Oh! They may try but when you meet him and love him it does not matter what others do. Nobody will have to tell you to Praise Him! I have been in some churches where the worship leader would tell the people to stand up on their feet to worship Jesus and some people would just sit there. Now I am not judging anyone. And I am not trying to put anyone in bondage. But when Jesus comes into your heart and life, no-one will have to beg you to get up on your feet to worship and Praise Him! For when you meet Jesus and he comes in to your heart and life, there is joy unspeakable. And there is Hope! And with joy we can draw water from the wells of salvation.

"With Joy I Draw Water"

With Joy I draw water
from the wells of salvation.
Thirsty and hungry for Jesus,
all worldly wells I shun.

Nothing can satisfy
in this wilderness we trod.
So with Joy I am drawing,
from the wells of my God.

Oh! I love the Lord
with all of my heart, soul and mind.
All other wells
I've gladly left behind.

There is only one well
where the water is fresh and pure.
Only one well that will quench
my thirst for sure!

Now I'll no longer thirst.
For there is living water in my soul.
I'll no longer want the wells of this world.
For Jesus lives in me making me whole.

We cannot survive without Jesus and the living water he offers us. We will shrivel up and die. People try to live without Jesus every day, but if they really tell you the truth, they aren't happy. Just like a plant needs water to survive, we need the living water that God offers us. One of my favorite Psalms is Psalms 1. David says, "Blessed is the man that walketh not in the counsel of the ungodly, nor standeth in the way of Sinners, nor sitteth in the seat of the scornful. 2. But his delight is in the law of the Lord, and in his law doth he meditate both day and night. 3. And he shall be like a tree planted by the rivers of water, that bringeth forth his fruit in his season; his leaf also shall not wither, and whatsoever he doeth shall prosper. 4. The ungodly are not so, but are like the chaff which the wind driveth away." David tells us right there how to prosper and be in health. We will be like a tree planted by the rivers of water. Just like a plant grows and flourishes with sunshine and water. We need Jesus God's Son to shine on us and we need to allow his Holy Spirit to flow in us and through us. We cannot survive without our Heavenly Father, without Jesus being our bread and without God's Holy Spirit quenching our thirst. No matter how hard we try to avoid God, we cannot live without him. We need him to shine on us.

"Shine On Me, Oh! Blessed Savior!"

Shine on me, Oh! Blessed Savior.
Shine on me forevermore.
For without the light of your presence.
I'd just shrivel up and be no more.

I need your smile to shine on me.
So precious Lord stay close by.
For without your light, I would be in the dark,
and there I would surely die.

Just as a plant needs water
it needs the light also.
To make it healthy, beautiful, shine
and also to make it grow.

Without your light, Lord,
I would not bear any fruit.
So in your presence, Lord, help me stay,
give me strength in this pursuit.

Help me Lord in your light,
to live and to abide.
And thank you Lord

for staying close by my side.

Help me always remember
apart from you I can do nothing.
For you are the Vine.
I am just the branch.
Help me never grumble nor repine.

And Lord when it comes time
for me to be "pruned" once again.
Help me remember Heavenly Father,
you are my Husbandman.

What you have created
you always take good care.
You know what you are doing.
You know more fruit I would bear.

And thus to the owner
it will bring glory.
And someday the glory
we will share!

We were created to glorify God the Father and do his will. And the only way we can glorify God the Father is by allowing Jesus to come in and live through us. And by yielding to his Holy Spirit. For in our flesh, our natural mind, we cannot please God. Only when we are born again can we glorify God. Only when we are bearing fruit we glorify God. Now I am not saying that God doesn't see our heart and our efforts, because he does. What good father is not pleased when he sees his little baby get up and take a few steps attempting to walk, even though that baby may fall a dozen times? But God does expect us to eventually walk. In other words he does expect us to grow and bear fruit. Jesus says in John 15: I, "I am the true vine, and my Father is the Husbandman. Every branch in me that beareth not fruit he taketh away, and every branch that beareth fruit he prunes it, that it may bring forth more fruit. Now ye are clean through the Word which I have spoken unto you. Abide in me, and I in you, as the branch cannot bear fruit of itself, except it abide in the vine, ye are the branches; He that abideth in me and I in him, he bringeth forth much fruit; for apart from me ye can do nothing. If a man abide not in me, he is cast forth as a branch, and is withered, and men gather them, and cast them into the fire, and they are burned. If ye abide in me, and my words abide in you, you shall ask what ye will, and it shall be done unto you. Herein is my Father glorified that ye bear much fruit, so shall ye be my disciples." Father God wants us to bear fruit. And what I mean by fruit is love, joy, peace, longsuffering, gentleness, goodness, faith, meekness, temperance, against such there is no law. Galatians 5:22. Have you ever been around someone who did not know Jesus, or if they did, it sure did not show. They grumbled and complained and were just plain miserable. It seemed like one minute you were all joyful and happy, until you got around them! And their attitude and actions and the things they would say would just about draw the life out of you. It left you sapped of your energy and you just could not handle being around them. Do you know someone like that? Or maybe it is you. Maybe you are one of those people. You are crabby, miserable and just plain grouchy. And people have often told you you are very difficult to get along with. No, you don't need a swift kick in the rear end, (like some have often told you). But what you need is God's river of life flowing into you and through you. God's river of life is what brings us hope, joy and life. Without it flowing into our lives, our homes, our churches and schools we are selfish, hard and dry. Oh! How we need God's river of life flowing through us flooding and overflowing every single area of our lives. Washing away every single trace of sin. Too often we allow sin to stop God's river of life from flowing through us. We can't afford to do that. We will shrivel up and die spiritually. We have to keep allowing his love and life to flow through us. We can't allow it to be stopped up because of unforgiveness, pride, strife or hatred or any sin whatever it may be. In John 7:38, Jesus says, "Whosoever believeth in him as the scripture saith, out of his belly shall flow rivers of living water." Jesus says out of our bellies shall flow rivers of living water. Rivers of Living

Water! Don't you want to be a blessing to others? For when we are a blessing to others, there is joy, peace, love, longsuffering, gentleness, kindness, temperance, meekness, and goodness. That is the fruit we have when we allow God's river of life to flow through us. God created you and me for this reason. As a channel for his living water to flow. His living water refreshes you and everyone you meet. You don't have to wonder why you were born or what your purpose is. Because that is your purpose. Letting him live in you by his Holy Spirit. Taking control of your life. Flowing in and out of you in a land that is dry, parched and barren because of sin. Surrender to Jesus if you have never done so. Ask him to come into your heart and fill you with his Spirit. So you can bear fruit to glorify God the Father. Heaven is counting on you. This world needs Jesus, will you take him to the world? There are many hurting people. People sorrowing over lost loved ones through death or divorce. People filled with hopelessness and despair. Maybe you are one of those people. Do you go through every day grumbling and complaining because you feel you have no purpose or meaning? Do you feel lifeless, hopeless and unloved? Do you go around saying all of the time, "Nobody loves me, no one cares about me. I wish I was never born?" After going through some tremendous trials in the past I have quoted those very statements. I mean let's face it, this world brings some really hard challenges. But the good thing is we do not have to go it alone. There is a Great God that loves us so very much! He created us. And he knows exactly where we are at and what we need. There was a woman a long time ago who knew what pain was. She knew the pain of rejection. She knew what it felt like to be kicked out of her home. Humiliated, confused and heartbroken. She sat down in her despair, when all of her resources were gone. She could do no more. She also had a son whom she had to provide for. She was in the middle of a desert. With absolutely no hope. Or so she thought. The woman's name was, "Hagar". She was the bondservant of Sarah, (Abraham's wife). She bore Abraham a son, named, "Ishmael". He was not Abraham's promised child, but a child of his flesh. You can read the story in Genesis 21. The child that was promised to Abraham was Isaac. Isaac and Ishmael did not get along. Sarah and Hagar had bitter feelings toward each other because of it. Sarah tells Abraham she wants Hagar and Ishmael out of their home. So one morning Abraham went and told Hagar that she was going to have to take Ishmael and live some where else. That was a very terrifying and heartbreaking thing for Hagar and Ishmael. Where would they go and what were they to do? I'm sure it was a heartbreaking situation for Abraham as well. But he had to keep peace in his family. You know what they say, "If Momma ain't happy ain't nobody happy." That's not really scriptural, but I had to throw that in anyway. Well, off they went with the bottle of water and bread and wandered in the wilderness of Beersheba. But before long the water and bread were all gone. Hagar put Ishmael on the ground underneath some shrubs and then sat down a good way off. For she didn't want to see her son die. For she thought it was all over for them. Then she lifted up her voice and cried. And the angel of God called to her out of Heaven, and said unto her, "What aileth thee, Hagar? Fear not; for God hath heard the voice of the lad, where he is. v. 18 The angel of the Lord said, Arise, lift up the lad, and hold him in thine hand; for I will make of him a great nation." Hagar and Ishmael were at the point of death. In Genesis 21:19 it says, "And God opened her eyes and she saw a well of water; and she went and filled the bottle of water, and gave the lad drink." Right out in the wilderness when they were at the point of death. Then God opened up her eyes to a well of water she had not seen before. Why didn't Hagar see that water before? It was there! But until all her resources were gone. Until she cried out to God that is when he opened her eyes to see. God opened her eyes. Had he not reached down to her first, she would have not seen that well. They would have perished! He reached down in his love and mercy and touched her. All Hagar did was cry out to him and he heard her and came. Are you going through a situation like Hagar? You've been kicked out, despised and rejected. When you know that God loves you and he accepts you it does not matter what others say or do. I know it hurts but when you realize God loves you and you are already accepted, it changes the way you see and handle things like rejection. We have to know that we are already accepted by him. Yes, he hates sin but he loves us.

"I'm Accepted"

You may not like me
or want me around.
But there is one thing
in this world I have found.

I have one that loves me,
no matter what I do.
He walks with me and talks with me,
the whole day through.

He's the one I aim to please.
Every step along the way.
He's the only one I want to hear
"Well-Done" from one day.

Yes I need to care about my fellow man
and others along this way.
But if you don't like me, Hey, It's Okay!
'Cause this world is not my home.
And I'll be leaving soon Someday.

So when others down here
are very hard to please.
And I get down and discouraged
and a little weak in the knees.
There is one truth that comes to my mind.
It helps me rest and my heart it really frees.

Is the truth that Jesus loves me,
and with him I am accepted.
He's with me. He's in my heart.
He's walking by my side.
And we'll never, ever part!

Hagar, when she thought she was all alone, feeling like no-one loved her, God seen her. All those years she served Abraham and Sarah. And now they don't need her any longer. What was she to do? She probably felt regret that she wasted all those years. She put her life into serving them and now they don't need her any longer. Maybe that is happening to you now. You may have been on a job for twenty years or so and then all of a sudden you hear, "I'm sorry, we just don't need you any longer." You are left feeling hurt, confused, hopeless, lost and even angry. Or maybe you have lost your job because of something stupid you have done wrong. And the guilt is just unbearable. God even cares about that. It does not faze him one bit. He knows about our stupid mistakes and sins before we even do it. He has already covered them! And know that when one door shuts another one opens. Just ask God to open your eyes to the "open" door for you. Only God can show you. Only God can open your eyes and show you hidden things. God says in Jeremiah, "Call unto me and I will answer thee and show thee great and mighty (or hidden things) which thou knowest not. Jeremiah 33:3. Then in Psalms David says, "The secret of the Lord is with them that fear him and he will show them his covenant." Some people may find it hard to believe that you can hear from God. And they may come against you on it. They may try to convince you that you don't know what you are talking about. What if Hagar had not believed she had heard from God? She and her son would have perished. David says in Psalms, "I had fainted unless I had believed to see the goodness of the Lord in the land of the living." When Hagar was in that wilderness God opened her eyes and spoke to her and told her what to do. She could have perished had she not believed. Jesus says in John 3:16, "For God so loved the world that he gave his only begotten son into the world that whosoever believeth in him should not perish but have everlasting life." Belief in Jesus Christ will keep us from sinking amidst the storms of this life. Paul says in Romans 8: 35, "Who shall separate us from the love of Christ? Shall trouble or distress or persecution, or famine, nakedness, or peril or sword? 36. As it is written, for thy sake we are killed all the day long; we are accounted as sheep for the slaughter. 37. Nay in all these things we are more than conquerors through him that loved us. 38. For I am persuaded, that neither death, nor life, nor angels, nor principalities, nor powers, nor things present, nor things to come. 39. Nor height, nor depth, nor any other creature shall be able to separate us from the love of God, which is in Christ Jesus our Lord." There is nothing that can separate us from God's love. Now we can allow our unbelief to hinder us from receiving from our Lord. So we have to get rid of unbelief and walk by Faith.

"Walk By Faith"

Though you may be sitting
and crying bitter tears.
Of all the heartache
of wasted day's and wasted years.

Our Lord will not let
one heartache or tear go unwasted.
Jesus will take and turn everything
around for good.
Jesus is good I have tasted.

You may say
things look too bad.
There is absolutely no way.
How things could ever get better.
But still you know you have to pray.

You don't see the miracle
with your natural eyes.
So quit trying to see.
In the natural what can only
be seen supernaturally!

It's by Faith
Not what it looks like.
It's not by sight.
So just know with Jesus,
Everything's going to turn out all right!

Because of Jesus we can go into the Holy of Holies. We can talk to God our Father anytime. When we get rid of unbelief and have faith, God will open our eyes and reveal himself to us. He loves us so much. And he went to great lengths to have a relationship with us. When we believe in Jesus we are born into God's family. He'll take us and hold us as a Father does his child.

"Our Heavenly Father"

Our Heavenly Father will wrap his loving arms around you. And say, "My child, Do not fear, I'm with you all the way. No matter what you go through. I love you always. I do not leave you when you are bad. My love for you stays the same. You're my child. I do not say, Okay you've been bad, you're not my child any more. No! I don't do that. You have my blood. Yes! I may get disappointed in you at times, in your attitudes, and your actions. And I may have to correct and discipline you. My love for you is the same. There is nothing that can separate you from my Love. I look at you and watch you grow. Sometimes it looks like you're growing real fast. And other times real slow. You have my eyes, my heart and my features. It's really special too, when you choose to obey me and to react to situations exactly the way I would. It makes me happy. I am so honored when you do. Because I've always given you the freedom to choose to do things your own way. It honors me though when you say, Father, I want to be just like you!"

I heard the saying, "Religion is man trying to get to God. And relationship is God reaching down to man." Hagar in her despair knew what it meant to have God reach down to her. He came to her and opened her eyes. If you are sitting there in your despair with your head hung down, cry out to Jesus. Give him all of your cares, your worries and your concerns. Give him all of your confusion. Jesus will come and tell you-

"Lift Up Your Head- Daughter of Zion"

Lift up your heads,
O Daughters of Zion.
Look up! Look up!
To your Father above.
Don't hang your head,
as if you don't have anyone to love.

You are my Daughter.
And I Love You!
Don't be worried,
for I will see you through.

Every situation.
That you don't understand.
Don't be alarmed,
for it's in my hand.

There's no way I'm ever going to let you go.
And if anyone continues to hurt you.
This you must know.
That I am your Father and you are my child,
they will reap what they sow.

So my precious, precious daughter
just rest and let me take care of you.
Just trust me and know
that I am carrying you.

Oh! Can you imagine the peace Hagar must have felt after the angel of the Lord called out to her from Heaven? God is the one that opened her eyes. He is the one that took the veil off of her eyes. So she could by faith hear him speaking to her. The Awesome thing is the veil is taken away for us today so we can hear God speaking to us!

"The Veil is Taken Away"

You've heard it been said,
Jesus is touched with the way that we feel.
He's touched when we hurt,
his compassion to us is very, very real.

But it's also good to know
that this great God, who is so High and Holy,
doesn't just sit on his throne,
and care only.

Oh no! His love and compassion
goes way beyond that.
He has come down from his throne
to be where you are at.

He's right there by faith.
We can touch him and he'll touch you.
So no more searching
there is nothing else you have to pursue.

For the one
you've been longing for,
is right at your hearts door.

Just acknowledge he is there,
and confess him as your Lord.
He'll come into your life and save you,
according to his Holy Word.

Let him into your heart

He'll come in to stay.
Let him touch you,
for, the veil is taken away!

When Jesus died on the cross for you, the veil of the temple was rent, completely ripped apart. You may say, "Well, what does that mean to me." That means we can go to God anytime, anywhere, just as we are. Paul says in Hebrews 4:14, "Seeing then that we have a High Priest, that is passed into the heavens, Jesus the Son of God. Let us hold fast to our profession. v. 15 For we have not a high priest which cannot be touched with the feelings of our infirmities; But was in all points tempted as we are, yet without sin. v. 16 Let us therefore come boldly unto the throne of Grace, that we may obtain mercy, and find Grace to help in time of need."

"I Come Before Your Throne"

I come before you my Heavenly Father.
With humbleness of Heart and Mind.
I come boldly to your Throne.
Your perfect will to find.

I love you my Father,
and need you today.
Teach me your will I pray.
For I can't make it alone, on my own.
I need you every second of the day.

I count it an honor to come to you.
Just to talk to you
and to share everything
I'm going through.

Thank you for being there.
No matter where I'm at, no matter what I do.
I cherish the moments we spend together.

I love sharing with you.

I Love you and appreciate you and
I thank you once again.
My Heavenly Father,
for being also, my best friend.

In Luke 23: 45 Luke says, "And the sun was darkened and the veil of the temple was rent in the midst. v. 46 And when Jesus cried with a loud voice, he said, Father into thy hands I commend my spirit: and having said thus, he gave up the ghost. "When Jesus was on that cross, before he died he took on all of our sorrows and borne our griefs. Isaiah 53:4 says, "Surely he hath borne our griefs and carried our sorrows; yet we did esteem him smitten of God; and afflicted." That is why he can have compassion on us. He carried our sorrows so we do not have to. He bore our griefs so we don't have to. We can go boldly now to his throne of Grace. So we can have grace to help in time of need. Then after he took on our griefs and sorrows, then the veil was taken away. Then Jesus died. The veil wasn't taken away after he died. The veil was torn when he took our griefs and sorrows, and sin. Then he died. Because he did that we don't have to go through any religious routine to talk to Jesus. Because he did that he has so much compassion for us. He knows how hard it is in this world. He knows how we hurt sometimes. He carried that burden to the cross. So you don't have to. No other man can have compassion on you like Jesus! We do not any longer have to go talk to any man to confess our sins. Because the veil was taken away. We can go into the Holy of Holies. In older times there was a veil in the temple that separated the mercy seat from the people. Only the Priest could enter in to bring the sacrifice for the peoples' sins. They did it once a year. They used the blood of bulls, rams, goats and cows. The Priest would sprinkle it on the mercy seat to make atonement for peoples' sins. For Jesus says, "without the shedding of blood there is no remission of sins.

"His Blood"

It wasn't the blood of bulls or goats.
That purchased my pardon, and set me free.
It was blood more special of a sacrifice,
that got a hold of me.

It touched me inside and out.
And changed my heart, my life,
my direction, without a doubt.

And this blood is still flowing
and healing today.
To whosoever will come
it's free, you don't have to pay.

You have to accept this blood
to get to Heaven.
It's the only way.
So hurry, accept His blood today.
Repent of sin and procrastination.
Come accept his blood, hurry without delay.

For his blood makes
the vilest sinner clean
and takes the spiteful
hateful and mean.

And turns them
into something new.
His blood is for everyone
me and you.

His blood has purpose, it does redeem.
Jesus paid it once, for all,
With his precious blood,.
To whosoever on him will call.

So we don't have to have
anymore sacrifice for our sin.
So into the Holy of Holies
we can now enter in!

It is only by the blood of Jesus we are saved. No one else can save us. It is not by going through some religious routine. And get this also, it is not by just going to a church building. You can meet Jesus and get saved, healed, delivered, made whole, and be brought out of darkness right where you are at. It does not matter if you are in your home. In a hospital room or motel room right now reading this. Or on a bus. In a plane across the ocean reading this right now, you can ask Jesus to come into your heart and life and wash you clean with his blood. That is all it takes. When you come to that place in your "heart" that you realize you can't make it any longer the way you are. You realize you need Help. You need a Savior. It does not matter where you are physically you can call on Jesus. You don't have to wait until perfect circumstances to meet Jesus. Call on him now right where you are at.

"It's in the Blood"

You may think you're a good person.
You try to do your best.
Well stop striving trust in Jesus,
and you'll be truly blest.
For life is in his blood.
So come to him all who are weary,
and he shall give you rest.

All you who are heavy laden
and burdened down with care.
Let it go. Give it all to Jesus.
For life is in his blood.
He will help all your troubles bear.

It's not by just joining a church
or going through some religious routine.
But life is in the blood of Jesus.
a relationship with him and on him you must lean.

It's not just by getting your name
on a membership roll.
But life is in the Blood of Jesus.
For only his blood can cleanse your soul.
For only he can write your name,
in the Lamb's Book of Life, on his Heavenly Roll!

John says in 1 John 2:1, "My little children, these things I write unto you, that ye sin not. And if any man sin, we have an advocate with the Father, Jesus Christ the Righteous; 2. And he is the propitiation for our sins; and not for ours only but also for the sins of the whole world."

"I Have an Advocate"

I have an advocate
up above.
He's pleading my case
always with love.

Yes, God hates sin.
And how it destroys
the hearts of women
children and men.

But if I stumble
and if I fall,
which I often do.
I have an advocate
who's paid for sin all in all.

So when the Accuser

comes to torment my soul.
My Advocate just tells him
all of my sins are forgiven
for on him I did roll.

My Advocate is not slack as some men are.
He's constantly watching over me.
This Advocate supports me without charge.
He already paid the fee, on dark Calvary.

Jesus my Advocate has paid the cost.
Once for all,
and the cost was oh! so high.
So thanks to my Advocate
I don't have to worry for He is always nigh.

Oh! Do you know what that means? That means you do not have to stand alone to fight your battles. You do not have to defend yourself. Jesus will be your Defense Attorney! Free of charge! Your fee has already been paid. Praise Him for that! For God says in Ephesians 2: 8, "For by Grace are ye saved through faith; and that not of yourselves; it is the gift of God; 9. Not of works, lest any man should boast." Salvation is a gift we have to receive. Like getting a Christmas present.

"The Greatest Gift"

The greatest gift for you and me
is not the presents under the tree.
The greatest gift of all
is to whosoever who will call.
He's ours for the taking.
The greatest present for others is not the cooking or the baking.
But sharing Jesus is what Christmas is all about.
We may not have money, but there is something without a doubt,
to others we can bring, we can tell them of God's Love.
That God has sent to us from up above.

Who grew like us to be a man from a baby.
Who died on the cross for you and me.
Receive the Greatest Gift of all into your heart.
He'll come in and you and him will never, ever part.

Many people go through so many rituals thinking because they do certain things it is going to make them closer to God. Like wearing certain clothes. Long dresses or maybe cover their head. They may pray to a wall certain times of the day. Or confess their sins and problems to a man on this earth thinking then their guilt is going to be taken away. People even think because they do good deeds, giving to the poor, they somehow have brownie points with the "Big One" upstairs. They may think Oh! I'm too good for God not to let me into Heaven. He wouldn't send me to Hell. There was a time when I thought I was a "good" person, I was probably going to Heaven. Then God opened my eyes to the fact I was a sinner on my way to Hell. And the only way I was going to get into Heaven was by trusting in Jesus alone. And what he had done for me on the cross. For there was nothing I could do to save my soul. No one has entered Heaven by just being good. You may say "How do you know, have you been there?" No, but I do know that it is all about believing in Jesus not ourselves. God's word says. In Acts 16:30, It tells about a time Paul and Silas was in prison. At midnight Paul and Silas sang praises to God and the prisoners heard them. And suddenly there was a great earthquake. So that the foundations of the prison were shaken; and immediately all the doors were opened, and every one's bands were loosed. And the keeper of the prison awoke and seen the prison doors open. He drew out his sword and he was going to kill himself. For he thought he was going to be killed anyway. Because Paul and Silas whom he was supposed to be watching escaped. Then Paul cried out to him before he killed himself and told him Do thyself no harm for we are all here. Then the Guard of Paul and Silas fell down before their feet. And asked them, what must I do to be saved? And they said, "Believe on the Lord Jesus Christ and thou shalt be saved, and thy house." Then the Guard took Paul and Silas into his home that night and washed their stripes, and

Paul baptized him, he and all his house. And that night Paul and Silas ate with that Guard and his family. They all rejoiced. Believing in God with all his house. That guard was at the point of killing himself. And Paul told him No, don't do that. There is Hope! Put your faith and hope in Jesus. Believe on the Lord Jesus Christ and thou shalt be saved and thy house." When someone is at the end of their road, no religious routine is going to save them then at the point of their despair. Only by calling on Jesus. And sometimes all we have to do is say, "Lord, Help Me!" Fourteen years ago I was totally at the end like that guard. And I cried out to our Lord Jesus. I said Lord, please help me. Take my life and use it for your glory. If you don't take control of my life Lord I will. I can't go on anymore! I was totally at the end of my self. I was lonely, empty and hopeless. That day I sat down and turned on my television to a Christian station. And a singer named, "Laverne Tripp" was on, singing with his family. I prayed that prayer with Laverne Tripp. And I asked the Lord to forgive me of my sins and come into my heart and save me. I said Lord please take my life and use it for your glory. I want to go where you want me to go, say what you want me to say, and do what you want me to do. I renounced Satan and said Satan you are not the Lord of my life, Jesus Christ is Lord of my life. Then I turned and got an old church hymnal off of the book shelf and just so happened to open it up to page 213. It says, "I'll go wherever you want me to go." The chorus reads I'll go wherever you want me to go. I'll say whatever you want me to say. And I'll do whatever you want me to do, I'll be whatever you want me to be." Right then Jesus was confirming with me he was in me ordering my steps. Oh! What an awesome thing he did for me that day. That was fourteen years ago. And since that time he has been in me, around me, behind me, before me. Walking with me, in me, and through me. He has brought me through some very difficult times. Before and after I met him. And no I did not say I have been perfect. But he's been with me every step now. And I love him and I thank him for his patience and unconditional love.

"We've Traveled a Million Miles"

A million miles ago,
I was at death's door.
A million miles ago,
I didn't want to go on anymore.

A million miles ago I gave
Jesus my hand.
A million miles ago he led me
across the Red Sea on dry land.
A million miles ago
Jesus led me through sinking sand.

A million miles ago.
Jesus took me out of the fiery furnace
out of the hot burning coal.
A million miles ago
He wrote my name in red on his heavenly roll.

A million miles ago
he opened the prison cells.
A million miles ago
I started hearing angel's bells.

A million miles ago
I started walking by faith on the sea.
A million miles ago
just Jesus and Me!

There's still another million I'm sure
just up ahead.
But with Jesus leading the way,
I have nothing at all to dread.

It was like one moment I was totally hopeless. And the next moment filled with Hope. Filled with Jesus! Filled with Life, wonder and anticipation. Like Mary when she went to the tomb after Jesus had died. She went to the tomb that day filled with sorrow, hopelessness, confusion and probably anger at what they had done to Jesus. She was probably empty and probably numb and in a state of shock. But then Jesus appeared to her at first in a way that caused her to not recognize who he was. Because she thought he was a gardener. Then she realized who he was when he called her name personally. Mary! Oh Then she knew it was him! Her Lord! Her Savior! Her Everything! Her All! Her Love! By his Spirit, (his resurrection power), she was lifted up. Or shall I say that sorrow and hopelessness and all that other negative junk was lifted up out of her. And now she was filled with Life instead. Oh how awesome!

"Yours Truly!"

I was living
such a wasted life.
Full of misery and shame.
I was empty, discontented.
'Til I called upon your name.

A friend of mine
had told me of you.
Of how you brought him through.
He told me how much you loved me.
I thought this was too good to be true.

But now I'm yours truly.
Forever and always.
I am yours truly.
I am yours and you are mine.
I am yours truly
No other Love like ours I could find.

Oh! Lord you've changed
my life completely,
with just one look, one touch.
I have tasted of your goodness.
There's nothing else I want so much.

And Lord you've been so good to me.
Since I've met you I've been blest.
And Lord I'll go. Anywhere you go.
North, South, East and West.

So Lord I just want you to know.
No matter where we go.
I'll cling to your strong arm and stay close by.
Lord you've touched my heart now,
nothing else will satisfy!

Since I have met Jesus, I haven't always walked perfect before him. But the difference is I have him and I am forgiven. It is not whether we are good in other peoples' eyes. What sets us apart is having him and his blood covering our sins.

"The Blood Makes the Difference"

The blood makes the difference
it's what sets us apart.
Only the Blood can cleanse
a sin-filled heart.

It's not by works
of righteousness which we have done.
But we're only saved
by the precious blood of Jesus
God's only begotten Son.

It's His blood
that makes the difference
we're saved by his Mercy and Grace.
For through his blood, he obtained
eternal redemption for us, he willingly took our place.

For we are all bound for Hell.
unless we have his blood applied.
For the Blood makes the difference,
that sets us apart, for through it, with him we abide.

Over the years I have had people turn their nose down to me because they thought they were so much better than I was. They would even go to church also. But because I would have struggles that maybe they weren't having or have never had. They assumed because I was having problems I was not God's child. People not realizing that their self-righteousness is not going to get them to Heaven are blinded to their need for Jesus. I don't care how good we think we are or have been we all need Jesus!

"We All Need Jesus!"

You may be a good person
that never has done wrong.
You're good and kind
and always with others get along.

Or you may be the wickedest one
that has ever been born.
We all need God's Grace
and never, ever scorn.

You may think, Hey, you've been good,
and you don't know what you have done.
Whether good or bad, we all need Jesus
God's only begotten Son.

We all need his forgiveness
and to be with his blood washed clean.
So whether you're good or whether you're mean
we all need Jesus and on his strong arm to lean.

For our righteousness is as filthy rags.
Jesus is the only Way.
So confess all your sin, whether you are good or bad,
humble yourself and pray!

In Isaiah 64:6 he says, "But we are all as an unclean thing, and all our righteousness are as filthy rags; and we all do fade as a leaf; and our iniquities, like the wind, have taken us away." Only when we are depending on the righteousness of God by faith will we be saved. Paul says in Romans 3:22 "Even the righteousness of God which is by faith of Jesus Christ, unto all and upon all them that believe, for there is no difference. 25. For all have sinned and come short of the glory of God; Being justified freely by his grace through the redemption that is in Christ Jesus." God says we have all sinned and came short of his Glory.

"You, My Lord"

You, my Lord took me in.
Even while I was dead in sin.
You loved me.
You made me begin again.

You took me in when
no one else wanted me.
You my Lord gave me
a reason to be.

You gave me hope.
And something to look forward to.
For someday,

I'm gonna leave this world,
and finally be with you.

You, my Lord,
are my Hope.
You, my Lord,
are my Joy.
You, my Lord
are my All in All!

We better be very careful if we compare ourselves to others. Jesus says in Matthew 5:20, "For I say unto you, That except your righteousness shall exceed the righteousness of the scribes and Pharisees, ye shall in no case enter into the kingdom of Heaven." What Jesus meant was the scribes and Pharisees was trusting in their own goodness and righteousness to make it into Heaven. They did not want to have anything to do with Jesus. In fact they criticized him all the time and persecuted him. They did not believe he was who he said he was. They rejected the only one who could save them. Jesus tells us a parable in Luke 18:9, "And he spake this parable unto certain which trusted in themselves that they were righteous, and despised others: 10. Two men went up into the temple to pray; the one a Pharisee, and the other a publican. 11. The Pharisee stood and prayed thus with himself, God I thank thee, that I am not as other men are, extortionist, unjust, adulterers, or even as this publican. 12. I fast twice in the week, I give tithes of all that I possess. 13. And the publican standing afar off, would not lift up so much as his eyes unto heaven, but smote upon his breast, saying God be merciful to me a sinner. 14. I tell you, this man went down to his house justified rather than the other; for every one that exalteth himself shall be abased; and he that humbleth himself shall be exalted." We need to really take a look at ourselves and ask ourselves which one are we like. That Pharisee who may live religious and maybe righteous. But then despise others. Or are we like that other man who could not even so much as lift up his eyes to Heaven. But smote upon his breast and cried out for mercy. Do we say we are saved by our righteousness or do we say Lord, I'm saved and it is only because of your mercy. Titus says in 3:2 "To speak evil of no man, to be no brawlers, but gentle, shewing all meekness unto all men. v.3 For we ourselves also were sometimes foolish, disobedient, deceived, serving divers lusts, and pleasures, living in malice, and envy, hateful and hating one another. v.4 But after that the kindness and love of God our Savior toward man appeared, 5. Not by works of righteousness which we have done, according to his mercy he saved us, by the washing of regeneration, and renewing of the Holy Ghost. 6. Which he shed on us abundantly through Jesus Christ our Savior; 7. That being justified by his grace, we should be made heirs according to the hope of eternal life."

"Nothing But Your Mercy"

Oh! Lord, I cried unto you
in my despair.
You heard me (with compassion)
for you were always there.

For you've brought me through
so many trials and many, many a test.
And you've brought me through the valleys
to a land of perfect rest.

You've brought me through many a test,
to help me realize.
When I come into the good land
not to get puffed up in my own eyes.

For it wasn't me at all
who got me where I am today.
For it was you Lord
your mighty hand every step of the way.

You were leading me
to the Promised Land.

Only by your Grace and Mercy
with you Lord now I stand.

For it was not by works of righteousness
or anything I had done.
It was only by your mercy,
and the blood of you, God's Son.

For you Lord initiated my relationship
with you right from the start.
It was you in your love and mercy,
that put this grace in my heart.

Oh! Sometimes it can be so easy to get self righteous and forget where we came from. We forget that if it wasn't for God drawing us to him by his love and mercy and for him opening our eyes to our need for Jesus we wouldn't know him in the first place. For if we do know Jesus, it had nothing to do with us. He initiated our relationship with him from the very start. 1 John 4:10 says, "Herein is love not that we loved God, but that he loved us, and sent his Son to be the propitiation for our sins." He loved us first, even while we were yet sinners. Paul says in Romans 5: 8, "But God commendeth his love toward us in that, while we were yet sinners, Christ died for us." Sometimes we tend to forget that when we see others that may not be as "good" or have lives as "good" as we do. We tend to forget God loved us when we were unlovable. I have been with a lot of people like that Pharisee. Oh! They wouldn't claim they were like that Pharisee. And they would get pretty offended if I said that to them. But their actions were like that Pharisee. I've rode with one on different occasions, different persons, and not that I am judging but they acted just like the one Jesus was talking about. Like for instance, we come up to a stop sign and there would so happen to be a beggar on the street with a sign that read, "I'll work for food." And I would tell that one that I was riding with to stop and I want to give them something and the one that I was with would say, "I'm not stopping and giving them anything.

They need to get out and get a job. I work hard for my money." That has happened so many times while I was riding with even so-called Christians. Whether we like to admit it or not, if we say things like that about someone, we are like that Pharisee. And we need to repent, and look at ourselves and people the way God sees us. With eyes of love and compassion. He Loves us All!

"There is Hope for Everyone!"

I saw a beggar on the street,
just the other day.
I could see his life of pain,
though a word he did not say.

I could tell, by the look in his eyes
of the weariness of his soul.
And I wondered how many others like him
need to be whole.

This world is filled with people
who need our Saviors' Love.
Heaven is watching
us from above.

Oh! will we tell them
of the Masters' Care?
Let's tell them there is light,
though there is darkness everywhere.

For no matter where you are at
even if in the depths of despair.
There is always hope for everyone
for our Lord is always there!

Too many times we look on outward appearances and judge whether someone is righteous or not. And just because someone is a beggar on the street it does not mean they are not a child of God. What makes us think that person is not already saved (born again)? Just because we may be blessed with a big, fancy house and car and have the finest of everything, it does not mean that you are God's child and that beggar isn't. Just because you may outwardly look more like Gods' child more than that beggar is, it does not mean that you are and God loves you more. Could it be that God may have given you more because he trusted that maybe he could go through you to give to the poor? Could it be that he wants to use you as a "Conduit" to pass his provisions, his love, his compassion, his blessing, his good fortune on to the poor? How do we know that that beggar on the street is not an angel unaware? As Paul says in Hebrews 13:1, "Let brotherly love continue. Do not forget to entertain strangers for by so doing some have entertained angels unaware. "How many times have we been like that Pharisee without even realizing it? Even in church, we want to sit with those who make "us" look important. Someone who comes in well dressed and looks like he has a million dollars, but then when someone comes in who doesn't look like he has much, we don't give them the time of day. James even talked about not having respect for persons. James 2: 1 he says, "My Brethren have not the faith of our Lord Jesus Christ, the Lord of Glory, with respect of persons. 2. For if there come unto your assembly a man with a gold ring, in goodly apparel, and there come in also a poor man in vile raiment 3. And ye have respect to him that weareth the good clothing and say unto him, Sit thou here in a good place; and say to the poor, Stand thou there, or sit here under my footstool: 4. Are ye not then partial in yourselves, and are become judges of evil thoughts? 5. Hearken my beloved brethren, Hath not God chosen the poor of this world rich in faith, and heirs of the kingdom which he hath promised to them that love him? 6. But ye have despised the poor. Do not rich men oppress you and draw you before the courts. 7. Do not they blaspheme that worthy name by which ye are called? 8. If ye fulfill the Royal law according to the scriptures, Thou shalt love thy neighbour as thyself ye do well." Jesus tells about a certain rich man, which was clothed in purple and fine linen, and fared lavishly every day; And there was a certain beggar named Lazarus, which was laid at his gate, full of sores.

And desiring to be fed with the crumbs, which fell from the rich mans table; Moreover the dogs came and licked his sores. And it came to pass that the beggar died, and was carried by the Angels into Abraham's bosom: the rich man also died, and was buried; And in Hell he lift up his eyes, being in torments and seeth Abraham afar off, and Lazarus, that he may dip the tip of his finger in water, and cool my tongue; for I am tormented in this flame. But Abraham said, Son, remember that thou in thy lifetime receivedst thy good things, and likewise Lazarus evil things; but now he is comforted, and thou art tormented, And beside all this there is a great gulf fixed: so that they which would pass from here to you cannot; neither can they pass to us, that would come from there." What Jesus is saying there is, not that just because you have riches that that means you are going to Hell. Because he doesn't mind us having money. He just doesn't want money having us. He wants us to realize that only he can get us into Heaven. Not good works, not our status in this world, and not even our money can get us into Heaven, and out of Hell! And it doesn't matter if you are rich or poor in this life. This Life is Temporary! It is passing, and if we are rich and don't know Jesus we are truly poor. And if we are poor and know Jesus we are truly rich! That beggar Lazarus that Jesus was talking about, knew he was not going to be like that forever. He had to have had the hope in his heart of Heaven, or how else could he have lived. He probably wouldn't have traded anything that he had for anything that rich man had.

"I Wouldn't Trade Anything"

I wouldn't trade anything for what I have now.
There is nothing this world could try to give.
That could be better than knowing my Jesus,
in me, he does now live.

For no amount of money
no amount of fame.
Could ever compare to my dear Jesus
and his precious Holy name!

God doesn't mind if we have riches. He just does not want them having us. He doesn't want us depending on money. He wants us depending on him! 1 Timothy 6:17 says, "Charge them that are rich in this life, that they be not proud, nor trust in uncertain riches, but in the living God, who giveth us richly all things to enjoy. 18. That they do good, that they be rich in good works, ready to distribute, willing to give to the needy. 19. Laying up in store for themselves a good foundation against the time to come." God wants us to always remember whether rich or poor this world is not our home. God does not mind if we have wonderful things he just does not want us getting comfortable down here. He wants us to always keep eternity in view. Because eternity does not start when you die, eternity is now. Where is your heart now? On the temporary or eternal? You cannot wait until after you pass on to get your heart right for eternity, you have to now, before your heart takes its last beat.

"Eternity is Just One Heartbeat Away!"

Some people may tell you
you've got your whole life ahead of you.
Live it up while you are young.
But you have to count all the money all the fame,
and all the fun and games, but dung.

For only what is done for Christ
and the gospel is all that will last.
That is all that is going to matter
so forget all the past.

Come and follow Jesus
Give him your life while you have today.
Let him be your friend, for Eternity is just
"One Heartbeat Away!"

Lazarus, I' m sure held onto the fact there was a better place for him. A land free from pain and sorrow, crying or tears. One time when I was going through a divorce, my ex-husband had come to pick our little girl up for the weekend, and his girl-friend came with him. I was so torn up. I cried so hard it felt like knives going through the pit of my stomach. I ran in the house and just stretched out on the floor. Just crying and crying so hard. Then I felt so lovingly like my Lord took his hand and put it under my chin and just lifted my head up. I felt his comfort so strong that day. And it was as if he was telling me, "It's going to be all right. Just keep looking up!" Then he gave me this poem.

"Keep Looking Up!"

When things below
keep me looking down.
My Lord whispers softly
and takes away my frown.

He reminds me
to always keep eternity in view.
He tells me to cheer up, my child,
sometime soon, I'm coming back for you.

He tells me keep watching
for I know not the day or hour.
He tells me he's coming back
in all his glory and power.

He tells me not to let,
the trials down here burden me so.
Keep looking up and keep watching
and when I come back you'll be ready to go.

My Lord tells me not to
let it hurt me when others do wrong.
He tells me keep looking up!

He will deliver me, it won't be very long!

He tells me very soon
there is coming a day.
When to everyone the deeds they have done,
he will repay.

And to those who are waiting.
And watching eagerly.
He's coming back soon
Keep looking up, he could come suddenly!

Oh! If this was all we had hope for, how miserable we would be! Because sometimes this world is so hard to live in, we can't forget:

"This World is Not Our Home!"

We shouldn't question the things
that happen in this life.
For the Lord is aware,
of all the sin and the strife.

For our Lord never promised
always a life of ease.
He said there will always be people
whom we can never please.

There will always be trials,
that would bring us to our knees.
But he did promise he'd stay with us.
He'd never forsake us, he never leaves.

So when things happen that tear our heart apart,
that we just don't understand.
Just remember we're not here for long.

We're just passing through this land.

There's a better Home awaiting
over on the other shore.
It's very close, closer than we think.
Just beyond deaths door.

And if you love Jesus
You're going to that Home above.
To that Land, where there is no heartache.
Only Peace, contentment, Joy and Love!

The enemy of our souls (Satan) wants us to keep looking down. He does everything he can do to take our hope and joy. He cannot stand it when we are living every day with childlike expectation for our Lord to return. He will use whoever and whatever he can to try to get our eyes off of Jesus! We cannot let him have his way. We have to keep looking to Jesus and keep Heaven in view! Too many times we get our mind on temporary things. On where we are going to be two years, ten years or twenty years from now. When we are young we can't wait to get eighteen so we can do what we want (we think). When we're eighteen we can't wait to buy a home and settle down. Then we can't wait until we get old enough to retire. We get older and get settled then we want to stay here and we get comfortable. We forget that time goes by so fast and we are not here for long. We tend to think we have a long time on this earth, but compared to eternity we are not here for long!

"Don't Forget We Are Not Here For Long!"

Sometimes if I get down and discouraged,
the Lord reminds me I'm not here for long.
He tells me I am not of this world.
That's why I do not belong.

My Lord reminds me he's building a mansion

up in Heaven for me.
And one day soon
That is where I will be.

Sometimes I like
to just sit at his feet.
And imagine what Heaven is like,
And Jesus when we meet

For it won't be long,
when all will be reality.
My earthly life will soon be over.
Oh! How awesome that will be!

Revelation 21 talks about Heaven. The three gates of Pearl on each side. The streets of Gold. The foundations of the wall of the city are garnished with all manner of precious stones. The first foundation is of Jasper. The second is of Sapphire. The third is of Chalcedony. The fourth an emerald. The fifth Sardonyx. The sixth Sardius. The seventh Chrysolyte. The eighth Beryl. The ninth a Topaz. The tenth a Chrysoprasus; the eleventh a jacinth. The twelfth an amethyst. And the city has no need of the sun or the moon. For the Glory of the Lord illuminates it. There shall be no day nor night there. And the Gates of the City shall be opened all the time. Oh! How wonderful it is going to be! The Presence of God for all eternity! Oh the praising, singing and worshipping God! A continual celebration! How Awesome! I don't know about you but I am so looking forward to it. Come on look forward to it with me! Let our Faith takes us there!

"Can You Imagine?"

Stop and Ponder just for a moment,
just how glorious it is going to be.
When these old earthly cares are gone.
And our Jesus we shall see!

Can you imagine
how good it is going to feel
when at last our Heavenly Home,
we long for now will be eternally real.

Can you imagine
How it is going to be.
To be finally reality.
Forever and ever,
Throughout all Eternity!

Can you Imagine
the joy we will share?
Are you ready?
Can you imagine you being There?

I don't know about you but I have such a longing to be Home! I have had my share of pain, sorrow and heartaches. And sometimes I just about can't take anymore. I've had my share of rejection when all I wanted was love. I've had my share of things happening that I just could not understand. I've had my share of crying late into the night. Because of things not turning out the way I thought they should. I've had my share of persecution from others who did not agree with me. So they persecuted me for being different from them. And all I wanted to do was follow Jesus! I find myself now with such a longing to be Home. And someday (I believe soon) I'll be there.

"Someday I'll Be Home"

Though I've learned
through a veil of tears,
to be content with what I have been given
through all of these years.

And though
I am very satisfied,
with knowing in my heart
my Jesus doth abide.

There is still a longing to leave
this world down here below.
There is still a desire and hunger,
for my home in Heaven to go.

No matter how content I am,
I guess there will always be,
a longing and sadness
to be home deep inside of me.

Someday I'll be Home
walking the streets of Gold.
But more than anything
I want my Father, me, to hold.

I have such a longing
to go Home deep inside of me.
I want to worship Jesus,
throughout all Eternity!

Some days I just sit on my back porch and just think how wonderful it is going to be to be finally home with Jesus. There will be no phone calls (telemarketers) during the time I am spending with my Jesus. There will be nobody demanding from me when all I want to do is spend time with Jesus. Have you ever felt like that? Where you just want to spend time with Jesus with no more being interrupted with the clock or with people (no offense) or projects that need to be done.

"No Interruptions"

One day soon
when my blessed Savior I meet,
for a Thousand years or more,
I'm gonna sit at his precious feet.

I won't be interrupted by trivial things,
I'm going to be with Jesus for ever and ever.
And no one on this earth
this hope I have in my heart can sever.

No one can take from me
what my Jesus has given.
So one day very soon
I will be liven.

in my home in Heaven
he is preparing for me.
And one day soon, I'll spend time with Jesus
throughout all Eternity!

Do you ever wonder how it is going to be when you meet Jesus. When it is finally your time to go into eternity? We think I'm going to do this and I'm going to do that. I don't know until that time comes. But you know it is probably going to be much like you are doing now. Don't ya think? Our Lord Jesus said, in his prayer when he was teaching us how to pray, he said, "Our Father which art in heaven hallowed be thy name: thy kingdom come thy will be done on earth as it is in Heaven..." So what we are doing now, pretty much is going to be what we are doing in eternity. Our Lord wants us to live like heaven on earth. And what is going on in Heaven right now? Worshipping, Praising our Awesome God and Savior! Singing, Joy and Laughter. A Celebration! No sorrow, no crying, no tears. No worshipping Self. Only Praising and Loving Jesus and glorifying God only will you find up in heaven.

"Oh! When I Get to Heaven!"

Oh! When I get to Heaven my sweet Jesus
I'm going to kiss you for a million years.
For all of the times you my Jesus
have wiped away all of my tears.

Or I may just hug you
and never, ever, ever let you go.
My Jesus I am so grateful.
So very grateful to you so.

Thank you Lord
for going to the cross, for me.
Thank you Lord
for setting me free.

I hope Lord Jesus
you'll be pleased with me,
to give me such a chance.
When I get to Heaven,
Lord with you, please give me
the First Dance.
For all of the time's
you've given me joy,
through every hard circumstance.

Or maybe Lord,
my gratitude to you I'll show,
By humbly bowing at your feet.
But how it is going to be Lord, only you know.

For Lord when I get to Heaven
for all eternity! Forevermore.
I don't want to let you
out of my sight anymore!

Now I don't know if that is really how it is going to be. We don't know until that time comes. I do know I am so thankful for him. I am so thankful that he loves me. Always. Once I was feeling scared that Jesus didn't love me anymore. I had done something, sinned in some way, I don't remember now exactly what it was that I did, but I felt so guilty. And the devil took every opportunity to accuse me. And I was beating my own self up as well. I really thought that my Lord was angry with me. See I had this mentality about the Lord that he loved me when I was good but if I messed up, he didn't love me any longer. That was so far from the truth. And I was really on a roller coaster ride with him. I was up one day and down the next. He has helped me see since then that he is with me, good or bad. He loves me always. And that just makes me want to please him all the more. I would tell him how I was feeling and he so sweetly and gently said,

"I Will Always Love You!"

One night while I was talking
with my precious Lord.
About the fear that was stabbing my mind,
like a two-edged sword.

I told my Lord about the fear
of him leaving me.
He said, "My child, I will never leave you!"
and that truth just set me free.

He reassured me that no one
can snatch me out of his hand.
He told me, that he keeps me
and by his grace I stand.

There is nothing I could do
that'll make him love me less.
He re-assured me he will love me always
and now, on him, I rest.

He wrapped me in his arms
and told Old Satan to flee.
He said this is my child,
You better let her be.

He holds me now so gently
and on him I rest.
He tells me just lay my head
here upon his breast.

He tells me he will love me
always and forever.
He tells me so gently and tenderly!
he'll leave me never.

Oh! I couldn't make it
without his sweet love to me he shows.
And knowing his goodness, my love for him,
each step grows and grows and grows.

He's my lover, my best friend
without him, I couldn't live.
So I lean on him
and my life to him I give.

Oh! How my life has changed
since I found his love.
For my Lord is right here with me,
no more way up above.

He is living in me
guiding each step I take.
Oh! What a difference
in my life, my Lord did make.

So you gotta meet,
this Dear Love of mine.
He loves you. He loves us all.
Look at the Cross, (His Love Sign).

Do you find yourself feeling loved when you are good and then finding yourself feeling unloved and scared when you do wrong? Yes, God hates sin and sin will be judged. But God does not love the way we humans do. One minute if someone is good to us we love them but then the next minute if they do something wrong we are ready to kick them out of our house and even our life. Gods love is not like ours, he loves us always. And if that was the case not a one of us would make it to Heaven, would we? As David said in the Bible "Oh! Lord, if you should mark iniquities who could stand? If we are going by our performance to make it to Heaven, we might as well hang it up. Because we are not perfect. We can only go by Jesus, and whether he has "written your name in his Lambs Book of Life". Is your name written there?

"Is Your Name Written There?"

Your name may be written
on the highest mountain.
For all the world to see.
But that is not going to matter
Nor make you a home in Heaven, for all eternity.

Your name may be written in Hollywood,
on the sidewalk of the stars
with the famous and elite.
But it's not going to matter nor get you to Heaven
or at the Marriage Supper reserve you a seat.

Your name may be written in the worlds'
Hall of Fame.

But it won't get you
through the Pearly Gates
Nor walking the streets of Gold, just the same.

There are so many places
we can have our name written down.
But only one makes a difference anyplace, anywhere!
"The Lambs Book of Life"
Tell me, Is Your Name Written There?

You may be saying, "What is the Lamb's Book of Life? I've never heard of that." You may ask, What difference does it really make if my name is there? Well, the difference it makes is Heaven or Hell. The Lamb's Book of Life is God's roll book in Heaven. And the only way you get your name in God's roll book is to recognize you need to call on Jesus. When we call on Jesus and trust in him to save us, and to wash us clean with his blood, he does just that. He comes in and cleanses us and makes us born again. When we become born again, God our Father writes our name in "The Lambs Book of Life." We then become citizens of our Heavenly Kingdom. We have hope of a better country. When we call on Jesus to save you, no longer will you be just going through this life just waiting on it to end and then you don't know what will happen. No, now you have hope. That this life is not all there is. You have hope of Heaven just as good as you were already there. What an awesome thought. If you have never called on Jesus to save you, call on him. Tell him you want to know him personally. He is the Way, the Truth, and the Life. You have to know Jesus to get to Heaven. He is the only one that can give you your reservation. And when you call on him and are born again, you will never be the same. This whole world will be different to you. Then you will be like countless others that are:

"Strangers In a Strange Land"

I'm a stranger
in a strange land.

I'm waiting for my pilot to arrive.
Here at the gate I stand.

I'm waiting and watching
for my call to board.
For this is one trip
to miss, I can't afford.

For this land, to me is foreign.
I have no desire to stay.
But if this trip, my pilot
chooses to delay.

There is one thing that I pray
that I'll take.
As many people with me,
and this world they will forsake.

To this world I came to work,
for this purpose my pilot brought me here.
He told me he was coming back to get me,
and for me not to fear.

At the appointed time
he will be back.
So please come on go with me,
your bags you won't have to pack.

Our treasures are up there
and not here below.
We'll call him and tell him
you also want to go.

We'll just call my pilot together.
and ask him your reservation to make.
He's so waiting to hear from you.
And that is no mistake.

To make this trip you have to call him.
So please hurry before it is too late.
He didn't tell me, when he was going to return.
He didn't give me any particular date.
He just said to be ready, to be watching,
to be working and to wait.

Oh! What an awesome way to live! When you have that hope, and live every second with the hope of leaving this world and being in a much better place there is no greater feeling. There is no high, greater than knowing Jesus and that knowing if you took your last breath, you would be with Jesus in Heaven. Sometimes we get our priorities all messed up. We think Oh! If I someday make it big and get a lot of money I can retire somewhere swimming or maybe work in our gardens, we think maybe that would be the ultimate. Oh! That is not all there is. If we are just thinking of this life, we are not truly satisfied. Sometimes we may have it a little too comfortable down here on this earth. And we tend to forget this world is not our home. This home is not our final resting place. We are all only:

"Pilgrims Passing Through"

We're just pilgrims everyone passing through.
This world of sorrow.
We're headed to another land,
it could be tomorrow.

But passing on is certain for all
And for some it could be today.
It's going to happen
Sooner or later, come what may.

So don't get discouraged
if things aren't going your way.
There is always hope with Jesus
of a much brighter day.

So if you're in a valley
and you're feeling mighty low.
Just remember if you love Jesus
Heavens awaiting, and there you will go.

However, there's another place awaiting,
called, Hell, if Heaven you do not choose.
Oh Will you win someday,
or will you lose?

For we are all Pilgrims Passing Through.
This world will soon pass.
We will be through and finished,
with our earthly task.

So don't get discouraged,
about all these earthly cares.
For our pilgrimage can be over,
any moment unawares.

So in everything that happens,
and in everything you do.
Remember and never forget, we are all,
"Pilgrims Passing Through".

You know sometimes it totally baffles me, why, when you say anything to people about the topic of death they tell you to be quiet and talk about something else. But how can we avoid the issue? And especially if we are truly ready to go to Heaven. How can we be quiet? Don't we want to take others with us? Do we not care if others are on their way to a burning Hell if they do not know Jesus Christ as their Savior? When Jesus comes into our hearts we can't be quiet about the things that he is concerned about. Which is telling others about his love and that he is preparing us a home in Heaven and to warn us that there is a Hell to shun. When Jesus comes in he changes your life! He changes your desires for the better. He comes in and takes away that cold, dead sinful nature and sets you on fire. As Jeremiah 20:7 says, "0 Lord, thou hast deceived me, and I was deceived; thou art stronger than I, and hast prevailed: I am in derision daily, everyone mocketh me. For since I cried violence, and spoil because the word of the Lord was made a reproach unto me, and a derision daily. 9. Then said I, I will not make mention of him, nor speak any more in his name. But his word was in mine heart as a burning fire shut up in my bones, and I was weary with forbearing and I could not stay."

Jeremiah was telling people the Truth. What the Lord was saying, and then all the people turned on him, and started mocking him and then Jeremiah said Lord you have deceived me how could you let this happen to me, I said what you wanted me to say, and now all the people are mocking me. Then Jeremiah said that's it Lord I am never speaking again in your name. But Jeremiah found out that God put that word in his heart, and there wasn't anything Jeremiah could do about it. It was just like he said, like Fire shut up in his bones! In v.10 of that same chapter in Jeremiah he says, "For I heard the defaming of many, fear on every side. Report, say they, and we will report it. All my familiars watched for my halting, saying, Peradventure he will be enticed, and we shall prevail against him, and we shall take our revenge on him." See, they were waiting on him to mess up so they could prevail against him, they wanted revenge on him. And in v. 11 Jeremiah cries "But the Lord is with me as a mighty terrible one: therefore my persecutors shall stumble, and they shall not prevail; they shall be greatly ashamed; for they shall not prosper: their everlasting confusion shall never be forgotten. "Jeremiah knew the Lord was with him no matter if anyone came to kill him and take revenge. He had assurance! He had God's Word in his heart as a fire shut up in his bones! Fear may have been on every side of him. But he knew that his Lord was with him as a mighty terrible one. Oh! How awesome to know that even if someone is coming to kill us. In 1 John 2:25 John says, "And this is the promise that he hath promised us, even eternal life. "Death may be knocking and you may smell it at your door, but when you have God's Word and his assurance in your heart. And you really know the Lord is with you, and you know you already have the victory over Death, there is no reason to Fear! And when you know when you take your last breath upon this earth that you will be with Jesus in Heaven, how can you keep that to yourself? If you really have that hope in your heart, and if the Lord is really with you, how can you hold it in? As Jeremiah said "His word was in him like a fire shut up in his bones." Maybe the problem is we aren't really sure. We're not really sure if we laid our head upon that pillow and didn't wake up that we would go to Heaven. Knowing for sure whether or not we are going to spend eternity in Heaven or Hell is a serious question in which we definitely need to be consumed with the right answer. It's so sad when people don't want to talk about eternity. Because it is inevitable that we are going to all be in eternity one day, somewhere. In one of two places. If we are not excited about talking about it now we better find out why not, now, before it is too late. Because it will be too late after we take our last breath. We have to make sure now! We have to have that assurance in our hearts that we are definitely going to Heaven when we die, now. For:

"Now Is All We Have!"

Oh! Don't you know
Time is running out.
It's passing every second,
every minute, without a doubt.

We're not guaranteed tomorrow,
while living here below.
Now is all we have.
So time from tomorrow
there's no way we can borrow.

For it isn't here yet.
We have no idea,
what heartaches or joys
tomorrow we shall get.

So we need to make the most
of each and every second.
Seeking the Lord and his will to find.
For we shall give an account for what we have done.
Love Jesus and you won't be left behind.

So are we taking the time
we have right now to seek salvation.
Do we know beyond a shadow of a doubt
with Jesus we are in relation.

Are you born again
and living for Jesus free from all sin?
Filled with his Spirit, cleansed by his blood,
pure and holy without, within.

Are you walking with Jesus
in his marvelous light,
for Jesus' return could be today.
Are your garments pure and white?

Are you watching and waiting
letting Jesus have his way?
Are you ready to meet him.
Should from this world you pass away?

Oh! Make the most of every second
letting Jesus have his way.
For Now is all we have.
For he could come this very day.

We are in pride and deception when all we do is plan for the future on this earth. Our retirement benefits and what we are going to be doing in the future. Now don't get me wrong, God does want us to set goals and plans, for the future, but he does not want us leaving him or eternity out of our plans. And to be continually focused on this temporary life. For:

"Today Could Be The Day!"

I'll care not what today may bring.
Whether sunshine, shadow or rain.
For my heart doth now sing,
Through this world of pain.
Because of the hope
that I have in my heart.
And to leave, to me, would be gain.

For one day soon
my sweet Jesus will come
to take me far away.
We'll go to our home
he's preparing for me,
and Today Could Be that Very Day!

James says in James 4:13, "Go to now, ye that say, Today or tomorrow we will go into such a city, and continue there a year, and buy and sell, and get gain: v.14 Whereas ye know not what shall be on the morrow. For what is your life? It is even a vapour, that appeareth for a little time, and then vanisheth away. 15. For that ye ought to say, If the Lord will, we shall live, and do this or that. 16. But now ye rejoice in your pride; all such rejoicing is evil ." God says it is pride and it is evil when we say we're going to do this or do that, we make our own plans. How do we really know what we are going to be doing or if we are even going to be on this earth tomorrow? Do we really know? God wants us to walk humbly with him, every step and that means to keep our eyes on him. And to follow him and get rid of pride. For we don't know the future, only God does. Yes, he tells us things to come, but we do not know what befalls us tomorrow. Peter had to find that out. in Matthew 26:31 Jesus said to all of his disciples, "All ye shall be offended, because of me this night: For it is written, I will smite the shepherd, and the sheep of the flock shall be scattered abroad. 32. But after I am risen again I will go before you into Galilee. 33. Peter answered and said unto him, Though all men shall be offended because of thee, yet will I not be offended. 34. Jesus said unto him, Verily I say unto thee, that this night before the cock crow, thou shalt deny me thrice. 35. Peter said unto him, Though I shall die with thee. Likewise also said all the disciples. Peter spoke in his pride saying, "Lord, Though all other men should be offended I never will." Many times we try to be tough, thinking we have the world by the tail. Thinking we have everything all figured out. We like to think we have every single thing under control. Don't we? We plan our days. We plan for our future. We plan when we are going to get married. We plan how many children we are going to have. We plan for our retirement. Oh! We think we are so smart, because we have it all figured out. The fact is, we don't know anything if we do not know Jesus and are not letting him have complete control. For he is the one that has everything under control. Peter in due time learned that fact. After he spent time with Jesus walking with him, and talking with him, he was stripped of that pride. After Peter denied Jesus three times just as Jesus said he would do. And Peter even argued with him on that saying he would not do that. Jesus went to the cross. Peter carried a cross of his own. A cross that crucified his self-will, Before that happened he thought he knew what to do in every situation. But he had to find out the hard way he was not in control at all. God was! Peter was very heartbroken after he denied Jesus, the one he loved. I wonder if Peter was thinking after that happened, Well! Lord you knew that was going to happen, why did you allow that to happen? Why did you let me deny you? You knew I was going to do that before I did it. For just that night at the Passover Jesus told them one of them there would betray him, and they were talking among themselves about which one was going to do that. So they started striving among themselves about which one of them was the greatest. I can hear them now, probably each one of them was saying, No it can't be me. I do this for Jesus, I do that for Jesus. I probably do more for Jesus than any of you do. I can hear each one of them comparing what all they have done for Jesus. Competing about which one was the greatest. And then Jesus explained to them, that the one that is chief among them is the one that serves. So right after they were striving about which one of them was the greatest, Jesus told Peter in Luke 22:31, "Simon, Simon behold. Satan hath desired to have you that he may sift you as wheat; 32. But I have prayed for thee, that thy faith fail not: and when thou art converted, strengthen thy brethren." And in v.33 Peter says to Jesus, "Lord I am ready to go with thee, both into prison and to death. I believe God wants us totally dependant on him every step of the way. And he lets us go through trials to strengthen our faith and love in him. Not in ourselves, but in him. Couldn't Jesus stop Satan from having Peter? And from sifting him as wheat? Yes, he could by all means. But Peter, afterward, probably had more assurance, faith and strength in the Lord's goodness and faithfulness, that he would not have known any other way. Sometimes when we go through temptations and trials, we think God must not love me anymore or he wouldn't have allowed this to happen. He wouldn't have allowed me to fail. He would not allow these rotten circumstances if he still loved me. We need to change the way we look at our circumstances. It is not that God allows trials and temptations because he does not love you. But it is because he loves us.

"Because He Loves Us!"

When hard times come in this world,
and you don't know how
You're going to make it through.
Just remember, your Heavenly Father
really does love you!

You may question just how come if he loves you so,
he allows all this pain, heartache and woe.
We have to remember because he loves us
he uses everything to make us grow.

He loves us too much, to leave us alone,
to stay like we are.
We are so special to him.
There is no greater Love, By Far.

He is constantly
never changing.
He always has one goal on his mind.
He's always rearranging.

Never leaving
anything undone.
He's working all things together for our good.
Using everything to make us like his Son.

Peter was so heartbroken he had left from following Jesus. And he went back to doing what he was doing before he met Jesus. He went back to his fishing business. Probably feeling so hopeless, lost and meaningless. Probably confused and feeling like such a failure. But all did not stay like that for very long for Peter. Peter found that hope once again. And he knew the Lord's Grace and Mercy now in a greater way than he would not have known any other way. Peter had now such an awesome awareness of our Lord's love for him, that he hadn't known before. Peter was probably so distraught after he denied Jesus and after Jesus died. That he had forgotten that Jesus told him he was going to rise again after three days. Sometimes, I believe we have a tendency to take our Lord for granted and forget that it is all God. Because we get excited we might forget that it was him to start with that initiated our relationship with him. It is all him that we want to know him and serve him. We might have a tendency to leave God out of what we are doing or we may fail to give him all the glory for what he is doing through us. I believe that is why God allowed Peter to go through what he went through. So he would realize, he can't do anything apart from God. And also he can't stop from doing anything apart from God. Because he said Lord I would never deny you! But he winded up denying Jesus anyway. Just as Jesus said he was going to do. How many times have we done that? We've said Lord I will never deny you. I'll go wherever you want me to go. I'll say whatever you want me to say. I'll do whatever you want me to do. But then we fail when we are put to the test. How many of us have failed the Lord in that way? Peter was probably filled with such remorse, regret, self pity and maybe self hatred for having denied his love, his life (his Lord Jesus). All Peter could probably think of was "Himself". Peter came to the end of himself, because he found himself doing the one thing he thought he would never do, and that was denying Jesus, his savior whom he loved very much. By all means I would never say go and do something like deny Jesus just to come to the end of yourself like Peter. But in order for us to experience God's hope, it takes coming to the end of ourselves. Realizing that we can't save ourselves. Realizing we are not in control. Now Peter is knowing Jesus not only as his Savior, but now as his Lord. Oh! Can you imagine how Peter felt when Jesus arose from the dead just as he said he was going to do. And Jesus told Mary to go and tell the disciples he was alive. He told her to go and tell the disciples, And Peter. He didn't just say the disciples. He said the disciples, And Peter. Jesus knew how Peter was not only filled with grief over his death. But he was probably overwhelmed with remorse and regret for having denied Jesus. Thoughts of how he failed Jesus on his last days on this earth probably haunted him. How could he live with himself, after denying Jesus three times before he went to the cross. He loved Jesus how could he do that, he probably thought. How could he let Jesus down, he was close to him? But it was all according to God's plan. God started a work in Peter when he first called him, back on that boat, and God was going to finish it. God does not start something and then not complete it. You may find yourself right now like Peter. You may have walked with the Lord, but something happened. You thought you were doing so good with the Lord, and then all of a sudden you have found yourself denying him. Thoughts of how you have failed the Lord are being rehearsed over and over in your mind. Well! Don't let them any longer, "For we have all fallen and come short of the glory of God." Romans 3: 23 says. Peter even! He was no different than us. And God started a work in you and he will complete it! A work to transform you into the image of his dear son Jesus Christ. He is faithful to complete it. Phil. 1:6 says, "Being confident of this very thing, that he which hath begun a good work in you will perform it until the day of Jesus Christ." God allowed Peter to deny him. He allowed Satan to tempt him, to make him more aware of his sinfulness and more aware of God's forgiveness, grace and mercy. That does not mean to go out and sin just to know his Grace and Mercy. God forbid. But if you have failed the Lord, there is hope and there is still forgiveness!

"There is Still Forgiveness!"

You can't get away
from the mighty hand of God.
Reaching way down to right where you are.
I don't care where you've been
or what you might have done.
You're never too far
away from God's Son.

Quit trying to pay for all of your sin.
For Jesus has already completed the task.
There is still forgiveness
if you'll just stop running and simply ask.

Look up and take hold, of a nail-scarred hand.
That is reaching to you in Love.
Don't look around at everyone else.
Look up, Look up above!

For there is still Grace in this day that we are in.
So I don't care
How awful and sinful you think you've been.
For that is why God
sent his only begotten Son.To pay for every sin.

So stop, repent, look up.
Whosoever will believe.
Ask, Believe and Confess.
And Salvation you will receive.

Peter found that forgiveness! Oh! Can you imagine how Peter must have felt. Probably feeling really discouraged, distraught while out there on his boat throwing his net. Feeling lost now, without Jesus. No hope anymore for the future. All of their hopes and dreams just died on that cross. For they had left everything. Family, homes, jobs, everything for Jesus. Jesus was their life! Peter and all of the other disciples were probably thinking, Well! What do we do now? They probably didn't feel much like doing anything anyways. They probably had no direction. One day they were walking with Jesus being a part of what he was doing on this earth. Filled with such hope and anticipation for the future and then one day they watched Jesus, their life, their love be brutally abused, tortured and murdered. And there was nothing they could do for him. How frustrated they must have felt. Their hands were tied. What were they to do now? But all did not end there. Jesus Arose! Just like he told them he was going to do. Oh! The joy they felt when they found out he vas alive. He arose from the dead. Maybe you have watched your hopes and dreams and life just die right before you. It all slipped right through your fingers. Maybe you find your self all alone, hopeless and lost, with no direction. You had high hopes for something and it died right before your eyes. You're confused and maybe even a little tiffed at God. You can't believe this is happening or has happened to you. Just as Peter and the other disciples found out and seen first-hand God's resurrection Power. That same power is present with us today. And that same Power can take our dead, lifeless lives and transform us and raise us up. In God's Word in Romans 8:11 he says, "But if the Spirit of him that raised up Jesus from the dead dwell in you, he that raised up Christ from the dead shall also quicken your mortal bodies, by his Spirit that dwelleth in you." Jesus Christ with the power of his precious Holy Spirit can and will raise you up. He can take your dead, hopeless life and give you hope, purpose and meaning. He can take any situation or circumstance that you are in and totally turn it around for your good, and his Glory. Paul says in Romans 8:27-29, "And he that searcheth the hearts knoweth what is the mind of the Spirit, because he maketh intercession for the Saints according to the will of God. 28. And we know that all things work together for good to them that love God, to them who are the called according to his purpose. 29. For whom he did foreknow, he also did predestinate to be conformed to the image of his Son, that he might be the firstborn among many brethren."

Just as Jesus interceded for Peter, he is interceding for you right now. And he is working all things for your good. Each trial, and every thing that we go through is transforming us into the image of Jesus. Paul says in Romans 8:17,18 " And if children, then heirs; heirs of God, and joint-heirs, with Christ; if so be that we suffer with him, that we may be also glorified together. 18. For I reckon that the sufferings of this present time are not worthy to be compared with the glory which shall be revealed in us." It hurts us when we come to the realization that we are sinners in need of God's grace and mercy. It hurts our flesh. We don't like to suffer. No one in their right mind likes to suffer. But our sufferings are not worthy to be compared with the glory which shall be revealed in us. Peter was heartbroken when he denied Jesus. He realized he was sinful and a failure. And it was all a part of God's plan and God's working in his heart. Imagine the joy the disciples had that witnessed Jesus' death and burial. When they had witnessed also his Resurrection. Especially Peter, when he saw Jesus for the first time after he arose. And Jesus didn't condemn him. Can you imagine the joy Peter had. The hope, peace and love he felt when Jesus forgave him. Paul says in Romans 5: 8, "But God commendeth his love toward us, in that, while we were yet sinners, Christ died for us. 9. Much more then, being now justified by his blood, we shall be saved from wrath through him. 10. For if, when we were enemies, we were reconciled to God by the Death of his Son, much more, being reconciled, we shall be saved by his life. 11. And not only so, but we also joy in God through our Lord Jesus Christ, by whom we have now received the atonement." What a happy day it was for the disciples and Peter when they were reconciled to Jesus that day. All that hopelessness and despair that filled the air, and filled their very lives it was totally dispelled that day. And was replaced with hope, joy, love and excitement. They went to the tomb that day mourning and grieving. And was met by an angel who told them Jesus had risen and went before them to Galilee. He told them to go to Galilee and they shall see Jesus. They ran to where he was at and fell down at his feet and worshipped him. Oh! The joy of being reconciled with him!

"Reconciliation"

You know reconciliation
is such a long word.
But it really is quite simple
haven't you heard?

Because God sent
his only begotten Son.
To reconcile us to himself
It is Done!

Accept Him
Thats all we have to do
He died for all,
Me, them and you.

And Jesus is no longer dead
but he's alive!
That same Spirit,
that raised Jesus up from the dead,
your life he will revive.

For he's the God of Reconciliation,
by the power of his resurrection
He's given us the ministry of reconciliation.
To proclaim this wonderful news,
all over the Nation.

So proclaim
it loud and clear.
For everyone
needs to hear.

That Jesus loves them,
And he wants to reconcile,
for the Lord's Day is near.
And we're only here for just a little while.

In 2 Corinthians 5:17 Paul says, "Therefore if any man be in Christ, he is a new creature; old things are passed away; behold all things are become new. 18. And all things are of God, who hath reconciled us to himself by Jesus Christ, and hath given to us the ministry of reconciliation; 19. To wit, that God was in Christ, reconciling the world unto himself, not imputing their trespasses unto them; and hath committed unto us the word of reconciliation. 20. Now then we are ambassador's for Christ, as though God did beseech you by us; we pray you in Christ's stead, be ye reconciled to God. 21. For he hath made him to be sin for us, who knew no sin; that we might be made the righteousness of God in him." Oh! to be reconciled to Jesus! It is an awesome thing. To go from one day having no hope and on your way to Hell. And then to be reconciled to Jesus the God of all love and hope and to have him come in to your life. And now you are filled with Hope I'm not saying everything is all rosy and you never have troubles, but now you have hope that you are going to make it through those troubles because now you have Jesus with you all of the way. Is that how it is with you? Have you been reconciled to Jesus? I don't mean you've heard about him. I mean have you been reconciled to him. It is one thing to know someone by their name, but it is another thing to really know that one. Their likes and their dislikes. To know them personally, relationship-wise intimately that is another thing. You may say Well! I don't know if I truly know Jesus. How do I know? Well, There will be a change when you meet Jesus. He is not just like somebody else we meet down here. Oh no! He is God. When you meet Jesus. There will be a change. You will either accept him or reject him. But you will definitely know it when you encounter Jesus. You may shrug him off as not being real. But in your heart you will know it. Paul was knocked off his high horse on the road to Damascus. He was killing Christians. Oh! He knew it was the Lord. He fell down right away and worshipped him and said, "Lord, Who are you? and What would you have me to do?" He knew he met Jesus. And John when he was on the isle of Patmos writing the book of Revelation, Jesus was behind him talking to him, and he turned to see the voice that spake to him and he says in v. 17 of Rev. 1. that he fell down at his feet as dead. And Jesus then laid his right hand upon him. Something happens in your heart when you meet Jesus. When we are born, we are all created with an emptiness in our hearts and that emptiness is for Jesus to fill. If you are feeling empty and hopeless you need Jesus. He will come in and fill you with so much hope and joy, When you walk in agreement with him and let him reign over you, you will have hope. For he is the God of all hope. Paul says in Romans 15:12,13 "And again, Praise the Lord, all ye Gentiles and Praise him, all ye Nations. 12. And again, Isaiah saith, There shall be a root of Jesse, and he that shall rise to reign over the Gentiles; in him shall the Gentiles hope. 13. Now the God of hope fill you with all joy and peace in believing that ye may abound in Hope, through the power of the Holy Ghost." And in Romans 12: 12 Paul says, "Rejoicing in Hope; patient in tribulation; continuing at all times in prayer." There are many people who walk around and claim to know God. But they act like they are hopeless. We say on our money "In God we trust." But yet we're greedy, we hoard, we go to psychics, psychologists, psychiatrists and just about everybody else except God for answers to our problems. We have affairs and commit spiritual adultery in our hearts against God because we feel lonely and unfulfilled and unsatisfied. We read our horoscopes, call every family member and talk about our problems but yet we claim to believe in God. What is the problem? We have to get in agreement with Jesus! For the Jesus I know satisfies. The Jesus I know gives hope, peace and joy. The Jesus I know is faithful to strengthen and keep us from all evil. If we want the hope God gives we'll receive it when we realize we do not have that hope. Because we are not in agreement with the God of all Hope. We have to come to that realization if we do not have hope we must not be in agreement with Jesus! Bottom line. We can't skip over that line to get to the next one. It's like we go along without Hope, lost, wandering and then we realize something is missing. It's like you realize you have no hope and without hope you have no peace and without hope and peace you have no joy. For there is no hope without Jesus. Then God comes and starts drawing us to him through Jesus by his Spirit. "For no-one can come to him except the Spirit of the Lord draws him." If you have realized you have no hope and you start wondering what are you missing? Or maybe you know of someone who just seems to be filled with so much hope and you often wonder what do they have: And how can you get that hope, peace and joy. That is God whether you know it or not working in your heart. He loves you so much!

"I Never Realized"

Until I came, to the end of my rope.
I never realized how much I needed you,
Lord Jesus to come and bring me hope.

Until I hit rock bottom
with no where else to go.
I never realized I needed you
Lord Jesus and you, I just had to know,

Until I was backed up
against the wall.
I never realized it was you,
who I really needed to call.

Until somebody came,
and to me, the Gospel did tell.
I never realized without you Jesus,
my soul was bound for Hell.

Until I accepted you as my Savior..
And I heeded your Word.
I never realized,
It was the Greatest Story ever told, ever heard.

Until I tasted the goodness of the Lord.

And his Grace and Mercy.
I never realized how good it felt,
to be delivered, to be free!
I never realized, But now I know,
How much Jesus Loves You and Me!

Jesus opens our eyes up to see our need for him and the hope he gives. For if we don't see our need we won't receive. When you go to the store usually you make a list of what you are missing at your house, that you are going to need. And then you go to the store and get it. We realize we are out of something. Then we go to the store, pick it up and receive it. That is how it is with salvation and all of what God has for us. Out of his love for us, he opens our eyes up to our need for him.

"Ever Wonder?"

Ever wonder
why we do the things we do?
Why do we witness and tell others of Jesus?
Thats the Holy Spirit working in You!

Why do we read God's Word with such strong desire?
Why do we do what God doth require?
Ever wonder why we do the things we do?
That's the Holy Spirit working in you!

For he's the one that puts desire
deep in our heart.
He's the one that quickens us,
and life to us doth impart.

He plants the seeds within us, and waters
and helps us grow.
Oh! How we need him
Oh! We need him so.

Ever wonder who opens our eyes,
So that we may see so clear.
It's no surprise
It's the precious Holy Spirit, to me, he is so dear.

Ever wonder, what sets people apart.
And them he does sanctify.
Well! Really it's no wonder it's the Holy Spirit
filling a heart when on him they do rely.

Ever wonder what makes someone
love and keep on loving.
After being hurt and being betrayed.
It's healing from the Holy Spirit,
when every hurt on the altar has been laid.

So if you ever wonder,
you've turned the right way.
For to wonder,
to ask, seek and knock, it's okay.

For to wonder,
that you must do first.
for wonder leads to desire,
and desire leads to hunger
and hunger leads to thirst.

And if you hunger and thirst,
God promises to fill.
So if you ever wonder
ask the Holy Spirit to take over,
and he surely will.

So if you ever wonder,
it's okay to do.
For if you ever wonder,
that's the Holy Spirit working in You!

The Holy Spirit comes and convicts our hearts of sin, and opens our eyes to our need for Jesus to be our Savior. By showing us our lost, sinful, hopeless condition, he calls us to come to him and give him our lost condition and to confess our sins and hopelessness to him. And he in turn gives us his grace and mercy and forgiveness. Have you ever answered his call? You will know it if you did.

"After He Called"

One day while living
a life that was such a mess.
Got a call from an old friend,
who asked me how I was doing,
and I just had to confess.

I had told him
How I was doing,
and to him all my cares, I did bring.
I was so glad, that he called me,
It made my heart to sing.

He had my address,
and then sent me gifts,
and told me to occupy.
He also told me,
I had no more reason to worry.
Every need he would supply!

This was just a taste
of what my good friend had done.
For since he called me,
the good times had only just begun.

He told me for him,
to be keeping a watch out.
For he was coming to get me soon,
without a doubt.

He said,
he didn't know
when that time would be.
But for me, to never forget,
keep watching and to always, always be ready.

He said I could trust him
He would surely come back.
For with his promises
He is not slack.

Now I'm no longer living
in fear and dread.
For since this friend
has called me, I have hope,
that the best is just up ahead.

For my friend is preparing for me,
a very special place, and with him there I will go.
My friends' name is Jesus. Have you met him.
Oh! Please tell me, him do you know?
Are you watching, and waiting for Him also?

God initiates our relationship to him to start with and invites us to come. Revelation 22:17 Jesus says, "And the Spirit and the bride say, Come, and let him that heareth say Come, And let him that is athirst Come. And whosoever will, let him take of the water of life freely.

"Come To His Throne"

If you have a problem.
That keeps you feeling low.
I don't always have the answers.
But there is, one thing that I know.

I may not come to help you,
or change the circumstance.
But there is one place, you can go,
give this place a chance.

It's a place where you are welcomed.
No matter who you are.
A place where there's no greater love,
no greater love, by far.

It's a place of love and glory.
a place of peace and hope.
A place where you take your burdens.
A place to help you cope.

This place I'm talking about,
is God's Throne.
It's for everybody God welcomes you.
You and you alone!

God has provided a way,
for you to come.Come to his Throne.
He gave you his best.
For you to come, to his Throne.
Come and be blest.

Come to his Throne.
Oh! He went to Great lengths.
He gave his only Son.
So you would Come.
Come to His Throne.

Oh! Come, Come
Come to his Throne.
He will wrap you in his arms.
in the name of Jesus safe from all alarms.

So if you have a problem with no one to talk to.
And you feel so alone.
Just bow your knee to Jesus,
He'll take you before the Throne.

You can bring your petition,
with thanksgiving, make it known.
So Come, Come
Come, Before his Throne!

In Isaiah 1:18, God says, "Come now and let us reason together, saith the Lord; though your sins be as scarlet, they shall be as white as snow, though they be red like crimson, they shall be as wool. 19. If ye be willing and obedient, ye shall eat the good of the Land: 20. But if ye refuse and rebel, ye shall be destroyed with the sword: for the mouth of the Lord hath spoken it." God says over and over in his word for us to come and come just as we are. He says even though our sins are as scarlet and even though they are red like crimson for us to come. He doesn't say for us to clean up first.

"Even Though"

Even though you've caused me
so much grief and so much pain.
Even though you've lived your life, oh! so vain.

Even though you've often wanted to go
on your own wretched way.
Even though you've never wanted to hear a word I say.

Even though you've ran away from me, so very far.
I'm still, still right there, where you are,

reaching down to you, in love.
I'm reaching down to you from above.

Do not fear, for I am meek and mild.
Oh! Hear me calling for you my precious child.

For you to come up higher.
Come on, get up.from the muck and all the mire.

You don't have to stay there
please trust me, I care!

For it's not as hopeless, as it might seem
I sent my son Jesus to you, for him to redeem.

I've heard it said religion is man reaching up to God and relationship is God reaching down to man. Many people do many things to try to please God. I am so thankful for God my Father revealing Jesus to me. Do we realize how fortunate we are? God is so good. Jesus says in Matthew 11:27, "All things are delivered unto me of my Father, and no man knoweth the Son, but the Father; neither knoweth any man the Father, except the Son and he to whomsoever the Son will reveal him." When we come to know Jesus we will know the Father. John 14:6 Jesus saith unto him, "I am the Way, the Truth, and the Life; no man cometh unto the Father but by me. 7. If ye had known me, ye should have known my Father also; and from henceforth ye know him, and have seen him. 8. Philip saith unto him, Lord, show us the Father and it will satisfy us. 9. Jesus saith unto him, Have I been so long time with you, and yet hast thou not known me, Philip? He that hath seen me hath seen the Father: and how sayest thou then show us the Father? Jesus is the Way, the Truth, and the Life. We do not know the Father if we do not know Jesus. Many people say they believe in God and claim to know him, but yet do not believe in Jesus. Or they may have heard of Jesus but say he was just a great teacher, or great healer. But if they can't say they know him as Savior and Lord of their lives they do not know him and do not know God the Father. For when we know Jesus we know our Father God. And it is all Gods' doing if we know him in the first place. In Matthew 16:13 Jesus asked his disciples saying,

"Whom do men say that I the Son of Man am? And they said, Some say that thou are John the Baptist, some Elijah; and others Jeremiah, or one of the prophets. 15. He saith unto them, "But whom say ye that I am? 16. And Simon Peter answered and said, Thou art the Christ, the Son of the Living God. And Jesus answered and said unto him, "Blessed art thou Simon Barjona; for flesh and blood hath not revealed it unto thee: but my Father which is in Heaven." It is all God who reveals his son to us that we might come to him and know him. It is all God who sent his Son Jesus so we could have fellowship with him. Some of the disciples didn't even really know who Jesus really was. Some said John the Baptist and some said Jeremiah or Elijah. They were going by what flesh and blood (other people) said about him. But Peter knew who Jesus was! Because God the Father revealed to him he was his only begotten son. Oh! How awesome to have revelation straight from God. Oh! It is one thing to hear of what others say about God. But until it happens in your own heart your life has not begun!

"Until he lives in you!"

You can hear of testimonies
of what the Lord has done.
But until it happens in your own heart,
your life has not begun.

You have not
begun to live yet,
If you can't say
Jesus, I too, have met!

If you can't say
He's changing my heart,
and he's given
me a new start.

I have to say my friend,

you must be born again.
For we are saved by Grace
through faith in him.
So call on our Lord Jesus
let your life begin.

For there is a new song being sung
all around God's Throne.
Only the redeemed
of the Lord to them it is known.

So if he
is not real to you.
Ask him to forgive you
and your life renew!

Is Jesus really real to you? Is he just someone afar off? Or do you know he is with you right there? Oh! I hear people who say they know Jesus. But yet they live very lonely lives. And they are still searching, still clinging to other people. And my heart reaches out to them, because Jesus is so good. And he wants them to know he is real. And I also want them to know he is real. He has been such a friend to me. He's been my Comforter, my Husband, my Savior, Lover of my Soul, Defender, Advocate, Provider, Protector, Lord, my Strength, my Guide, my Hope, my Anchor, my Counselor, my Bodyguard, my Shield, my Commander, my Hero, and my Constant Companion. Oh! and also my Lawyer, Best Friend, Banker and Agent, my Boss, my Treasurer, stock broker and Adviser. And I want everyone to know Jesus in those ways as well. And I know I can say more.

"Oh! I Want You To Know Him!"

Years ago, while in my sin
full of shame of where I'd been.
Didn't have no hope ahead.

By Old Satan I was led.

Took a look at where I was
and where in eternity I would be.
I knew in Hell, there was a place
especially for me.

So I cried out to Jesus,
who in my head I heard about.
Let him in my heart
He's in me now without a doubt.

The Holy Spirit came
and led me to the cross.
Everything I've done
I now count but loss.

For I Glory now in Jesus,
and what he's done for me.
Oh! I am so grateful,
of all he's done for me.

I want so bad for others
to know my Jesus too.
For if it wasn't for Jesus
I don't know what I would do.

Oh! I want you to know him.
Let me introduce you today.
Just ask him in,
let him have his way.

Don't run from him be thankful.
He cares about your soul.
You won't regret it,
when on him your burdens roll.

Oh! I want you to know him
intimately.
He is so good.
He wants to set you free.

Oh! I want you to know him.
He will never let you down.
Full of Grace and Mercy,
Is He, I have found.

In Ephesians 1: 15 Paul says, "Wherefore I also, after I heard of your faith in the Lord Jesus, and love unto all the saints, Cease not to give thanks for you, making mention of you in my prayers: 17. That the God of our Lord Jesus Christ, the Father of Glory may give unto you the Spirit of Wisdom and revelation in the knowledge of him: 18. The eyes of your understanding (heart) being enlightened; that ye may know what is the Hope of his calling, and what the riches of the glory of his inheritance in the saints; And what is the exceeding greatness of power, to us-ward who believe, according to the working of his mighty power, 20. Which he wrought in Christ when he raised him from the dead, and set him at his own right hand in the heavenly places, 21. Far above all principality and power, and might, and dominion and every name that is named, not only in this work but also in that which is to come: 22. And hath put all things under his feet, and gave him to be the head over all things to the church. 25. Which is his body, the fulness of him that filleth all in all." Paul prayed for those people. He said he ceased not to pray. in Luke 18:1 Jesus tells a parable, "And he spake a parable unto them to this end, that men ought always to pray and not to faint; saying, There was in a city a judge, which feared not God, neither respected man: And there was a widow in that city; and she came unto him, saying Avenge me of mine adversary. And he would not for a while, but afterward he said within himself, though I fear not God, nor regard man. Yet Because this widow troubleth me, I will avenge her, lest by her continual coming she weary me, And the Lord said, Hear what the unjust judge saith, and shall not God avenge his own elect, which cry day and night unto him, though he bear long with them? I tell you that he will avenge them speedily. Nevertheless, when the Son of Man cometh, shall he find faith on the earth?" We need to pray and not faint. Paul ceased not to pray day and night. Do We pray for others like that?

"Not A Day Goes By!"

Not a day goes by,
that I don't lift you up in prayer.
I go talk to my Heavenly Father
for he is always there.

Not a day goes by, that I don't bring
your name before God's Throne.
So don't ever feel forsaken, unloved, unwanted,
discouraged, hopeless or alone.

And when going through trials don't ever think,
does anyone really care?
You have unseen friends though with natural eyes
can't see them, they are surely there.

They are the Father, Son and Holy Ghost.
They are always with you
waiting for your burdens to bear.
There's no place we can be alone.
The highest mountain or lowest valley.
For they are everywhere.

There is also a heavenly host
of mighty warring angels, fighting for us when we call
on the Lords precious name.
Not to mention a big, big family.
Who our Father loves each and everyone the same.

He loves us all.
And don't ever forget
in the times you feel lonely and blue,
not a day goes by that I don't pray for you.
And remember and don't ever forget,
Jesus really does Love You!

We all probably know of someone who is going through hard times right now. It may even be us. And we may not know of anything we can do. The situation may look totally hopeless. But there is one thing we can do, and that is Pray. There is always Hope when we pray. And keep on praying and not faint. Prayer really does make a difference!

"Prayer Makes a Difference!"

So many hopeless people
all around us where we live.
Prayer makes the difference
in a life all marred with sin.
If it weren't for prayer
I don't know where I would've been.

For someone took my name to God.
When without God, and on my own
someone cared enough to take me,
to the Father's Throne.

There are many people
in this world today,
who are going down a sinful road
going the wrong way.
One thing we can do for them
to show them that we care.
Is get alone with God today,
and simply Pray!

Elijah prayed and interceded
to show God's Power,
to Israel and to the Prophets of Baal.
God answered.
Prayer makes a difference
to save loved ones from Hell.

Prayer will make a difference
in this world today.
We may not see it instantly.
But the answer is on the way.

Pray to the Father
Pray secretly.
He will reward you
Reward you openly.

Prayer always makes a difference
Pray by faith and you will see.
Prayer makes a difference
for you and me!

If people would really get ahold of the fact that God hears us when we pray it would take away their loneliness. They say all the time I'm so lonely. And it is sad to say but it comes from a heart of unbelief. If they would believe Jesus is there and he does hear them every time they prayed they would never feel lonely again. If we would just take advantage of the times we are alone and then get alone with Father God, our lives would definitely be changed for the better. This world would be different. For God says when we pray to go into your room and shut the door. And pray in secret and when God hears you and sees you talking to him in secret, he will reward you openly. Satan the enemy of our souls, blinds our eyes from understanding that God hears our prayers whether we see him or feel him there or not. He is there, and we have to know that by faith and not by sight. As Paul prayed I pray that the eyes of your understanding be enlightened; that ye may know what is the hope of his calling and what the riches of the glory of his inheritance in the saints is. I pray that God the Father would give you Revelation of him, and the Spirit of Wisdom, for you have to know in your heart that Jesus hears your prayers. For how can we have a relationship with him if we doubt he is there and if we doubt he listens to us when we pray. What kind of relationship would that be any way? You have to know in your heart:

"Your Prayers Are Heard!"

Don't take lightly that prayer that you said.
For our Lord has heard your every cry.
For he is working even now, to bring your answer.
On him you can rely!

For your prayers haven't
fell on deaf ears.
He has heard and he's bottled,
everyone of your tears.

Oh! He loves you
so very much.
And those very problems
You can trust him to touch.

He's heard your cries and your petition.
He is definitely working it out,
to bring it to pass, what you ask,
without a doubt.

And never forget that he is faithful.
.He is kind and He is True.
He never, ever takes
his eyes off of you!

There is no greater joy than to know Jesus and to know he hears you when you talk to him. He does not ever turn a deaf ear to you. He never turns you away. Rest assured he has heard your prayers and he is working even now to bring that one in. And to answer your every need!

"This is to all the Mother's Who Pray"

This is to all the Mother's
who pray for their children.
They hurt for them,
who are lost in their sin.

They grieve for their souls
that have gone astray.
This is to all the
Mother's who pray.

Jesus sees your tears
and the pain that you bear.
He's right there with you,
he really does care.

He's moved with compassion
for your loved one's
who are lost.
Oh! Don't forget, for their souls
He's paid a high cost.

He loves them more,
than you can ever imagine.
Even though they are running
and living in their sin.

Jesus sees your heart
that's been so broken.
Just trust him.
He's working to bring that one in.

So don't you worry
Little Momma.
They're in the palm
of his nail-pierced hand.
And all around those loved ones,
is an unseen angel band.

So you just keep right on praying,
for it's never, ever in vain.
Jesus hears your cries
he understands your heartache,
he understands your pain.

So don't you worry Little Momma.
They're in the palm of his nail-pierced hand.
And all around those loved ones,
is an unseen Angel Band.
And all around those loved ones.
is an unseen Angel Band.

You know we have a tendency to forget when we are praying for our loved ones, that Jesus loves them more than we do. I know sometimes that it is hard to imagine but he does. He has died for them. He is really more concerned about their souls than we are. You and I may say that just can't be possible but it is. Our loved ones are constantly on his heart. He is in heaven right now and constantly making intercession for them, and for us all. Hebrews 7:25 says, "Wherefore he is able also to save them to the uttermost that come unto God by him, seeing he ever liveth to make intercession for them." Jesus Christ is able to save to the uttermost. For he ever liveth to make intercession for us. Take Courage and Comfort for Jesus is praying for you and your loved ones. There were times when I would start to feel alone. I would tell the Lord I pray for everyone else but nobody is there to pray for me. But it didn't matter really, for Jesus was. He was praying for me. So if you are feeling like that right now. Feeling like, I do a lot for other people all of the time, but nobody does anything for me. Well! Don't let self-pity get the best of you. Because Jesus loves you and is praying for you.

"Jesus' Prayer"

I'm seated at the right hand
of the Father making intercession for all.
And this is my prayer,
Oh! That all would heed my call.

Oh! How my heart beats and longs
for them to know me.
This is my prayer that everyone,
would choose to be set free.

I pray everyone with me
would be one.
And they perfect in one be made.
Just as I and my Father are one.

For there is only one thing to separate us.
And the debt I have already paid
There is nothing between us any longer.
The atonement for sin I have made.

This is my prayer
that all the world will see.
That they may know,
That my Father loves them as he hath loved me.

This is my prayer that the love
my Father and I have would so greatly burn
deep in their hearts within.

Purging out the dross purifying their hearts.
That they would be free, from the burden of sin.

I pray that all be washed in my blood.
Be Pure, Holy and Sincere.
That they with
their spiritual ears would hear.

Oh! I pray that all would have
the urgency of my heart,
that all would know I am real.
And that I am coming soon to claim my own.
Oh! The urgency I have I pray they feel.

I pray they
walk in wisdom redeeming the time,
and know the urgency of the hour.
I pray my Spirit out of them he would flow.
And they would walk in his Mighty Power.

So I through them upon the earth
would be glorified.
I pray earnestly and always
that they would all be satisfied.

Oh! This is my Prayer, always and forever.
This prayer will never cease,
until they are with me in Heaven.
And from the burden of Earth,
them I will finally release!

Jesus is seated right now at the right hand of the Father making intercession for us all. He is praying that all would heed his call, and know him. He prays that everyone would be free. And that with him be one. He prays that the love the Father and he has would burn in our hearts deep within. He prays that we would be pure, holy and sincere. He wants us to have that same urgency in our hearts as he does. He prays that we would understand the urgency of the hour. His prayer should be our prayer as well. When we know someone, and have a relationship with them and are committed to them, their troubles become our troubles. Their loves become our loves, their dislikes our dislikes, their desires should become our desires. And their burdens our burdens.

Jesus is Real! He is not just a figment of our imagination. He is the Son of the Living God. We can't just think positively and think we are going to make it to Heaven and leave Jesus out. He is our only way to Heaven to eternal life. It's all about Jesus. I Timothy 2:5 says, "For there is one God, and one mediator between God and men, the man Christ Jesus: Who gave himself a ransom for all, to be testified in due time."

We put our hope and trust in so many things that are not going to help us. We wish upon a star. We make a wish when we blow out our candles on a Birthday cake. We take our children to sit on Santa's lap and tell him what they want for Christmas. We put all of our extra money and trust in Lotto tickets and we try to justify it by saying it is going for the schools. We invest in the stock market. We even put our hope and trust in our paychecks. Which most of us don't even make enough to make it from Paycheck to paycheck in the first place. Why not put all of our hope and trust in Jesus. What has all those other things done for us. What has the Government done for us? We put our hope and trust in Welfare and Food-stamps. What have they really done for us? Other than keep us in bondage to them. It just keeps you from fulfilling your purpose on this earth and it keeps you from reaching your full potential. For you do have potential! You do have a Destiny! You do have a Purpose! Don't put your trust in things that bring false hope. You need real Hope. And the only real hope you are going to find is in Jesus Christ the Savior and Lover of your soul. Are you having problems and you're just wishing for something to change. Don't wish upon a star. Don't just hope your dreams are going to come true by blowing out your candles on your birthday cake. Who ever came up with that anyway? And please don't go to Santa and sit on his lap. And tell him what you want. He's not going to give you anything. He is a man in a costume with a fake beard. Who is going to forget everything everyone just told him. You may say this sounds harsh. You're taking all of our hope and don't tell my children that Santa isn't real. You are Cruel! Let them believe what they want to believe if it makes them happy. Is that what you are saying right now to me? If we really love our children don't we want them to have Real Hope? We don't want them to have False Hope. We want them to know Jesus. We need to teach our children to pray to God and tell him what they want. Not Santa! Jesus wants us to know and to teach our children to know him. He wants us to put all of our hope in Him. There is nothing we can depend on, to put our trust in, except for Jesus. Everything else will let us down. Are you putting your hope in the Government, Welfare, Food-stamps, Government checks? Don't count on them to always protect and provide for you. Only our Father God can we truly trust in to provide for us. God will snatch us out of whatever we are trusting in or putting our hope in other than him. God gave me these two verses when that what I was putting my trust in other than God was suddenly snatched from me. The first verse was Isaiah 57:1, "The righteous perisheth, and no man takes it to heart: and merciful men are taken away, none considering that the righteous is taken away from the evil to come." Don't fear if what you have been trusting in has been snatched from you. God is in control. He sees the future. And maybe he is trying to get you to totally trust Him. He is the only one you can depend upon. If you are finding yourself sitting there wondering what are you going to do now, remember he loves you. And he doesn't want you being yoked to anything but him and his anointing! If we don't learn that in little things, what are we going to do when big things come up? Another verse he gave me was Revelation 18:4, "And I heard another voice from Heaven, saying, Come out of her, my people, that ye be not partakers of her sins, and that ye receive not of her plagues. For her sins have reached unto Heaven, And God hath remembered her iniquities."

It's not enough to just wish and just hope for your problems to go and your dreams to be fulfilled. You have to get tired of living like you are living. And be determined not to settle. And get up and start moving with God, out of that place you are in. It is not enough to just sit around and scratch your belly and flip our remotes and say yea, I'd like a change in my life. Anything else we could put our hope in takes from us. But if you put your hope in God, he will give to you.

Yes, there are times when we have to make sacrifices but it is only so God can give back to us. The only thing he will take from you is your burdens, your troubles, your heartaches. Let him have your life, your hopes, your dreams, and your cares. And he will give you his life, his hopes, his dreams, his cares, his burdens.He is waiting there with open arms, to love you, to care for you. But you have to move and come to him. He will not force you. Hear him saying to you, "Come unto me, All ye that labor and are heavy laden, and I will give you rest. Take my yoke upon you, and learn of me, for I am meek and lowly in heart; and ye shall find rest unto your souls, for my yoke is easy and my burden is light." You know people sometimes when you try to witness to them of Jesus, it's like they act like they are going to get the bad end of a deal or something. They sometimes say, that God is just a crutch people lean on. And sometimes I've talked to people who say they don't want to hear about Jesus, tell me some other way to get out of my problems. They'll sit there and talk about their problems, their troubles and cares. And glorify Satan the whole time without realizing it. But then you try to tell them of Jesus and how he can change their lives but they don't want to hear that. They'll tell you they are not ready. That they are doing fine without him. That they don't need him yet. And it is so sad because what is it going to take to make us realize that he is the one that gets the bad end of the deal with us! I mean who do we think we are? We are the ones that miss out when we don't come to him. We are the ones that need him. Let's look at this picture. He gets us, all of our problems, troubles, burdens, cares, heartaches and broken pieces. He gets also our limited hopes and dreams, wants and desires. We give him our limited talents, abilities, skills, and our limited wisdom, creativity and our limited availability (for we don't have much time). See, we give him all of that in exchange for Him. The God of all Creation! The owner of everything, (our breath, our life, our time, our resources and yes all silver and gold is His! We receive in exchange: his life, his burdens, his desires, his abundance, and his provision. Not to mention we receive his security, his presence, his goals, his ability, his availability, and his protection. And I know this sounds repetitive, but the list goes on and on. We receive his hopes, his desires, his dreams, his cares, his concerns, his likes, his dislikes, his wisdom, his creativity, his passion, and his awesome power. And also (I am going to say the rest of these, whether it is repetitive or not). Also his strength, his comfort, his counsel, his skills, his love, his compassion, his rest and his yoke. And I probably can think of a bunch more. Now tell me which one gets the better end of the deal? Definitely We do! Are you burdened down with the cares of this life, and are you laboring and are heavy laden? Let Jesus take your cares and burdens and he'll give you his. And his burdens are light. You may be saying, "I didn't think Jesus had any burdens, he is God." Yes, he is God but he does have burdens. He is very, very real. He has a body, heart, breath, blood, life, concerns, desires, likes, dislikes, needs, hungers and burdens. He has a heart for hurting, burdened people that need him. David says in Psalms 34:17, "The Righteous cry and the Lord heareth, and delivereth them out of all their troubles. 18. The Lord is near unto them that are of a broken heart; and saveth such as be of a crushed spirit." Are you broken hearted today? Are you crushed in spirit? Take comfort. The Lord is right there with you. He hears your hearts' cries. Here is a song the Lord give me.

"The Righteous Cry"

He's been watching over me.
He's been watching over me.
He's been watching over me.
He's been watching over me.
There's been times of trouble in my life.
There's been heartache, trials and strife.
But my Lord's been faithful to watch over me.
Oh! He never takes his eyes off of me.

Oh! His eyes are over the righteous of the land.
and His ears are open wide.
He sees their tears and he wipes them dry.
His ears are open to their cry.

There's been times when my heart
has been broken in two.
By a careless word or two.
But My Lord has heard my humble plea.
when I cried Lord set me free.

Oh! His eyes are over the righteous of the Land.
And his ears are open to their cry.
He sees their tears and he wipes them dry.
His ears are open wide.

So if your heart is breaking into.
And you hurt so bad.
Just call out to Jesus on him you can rely.
His ears are open to his little child's cry.
He'll take that hurt all away.
when you just go to him and pray.

He'll hold you and love you
like none other can.
For his eyes are over
the righteous of the Land.

The Lord loves us all, but especially loves those that are poor, rejected and outcasts. David says in Psalms 35: 9 "And my soul shall be joyful in the Lord: it shall rejoice in his salvation. 10. All my bones shall say, Lord, who is like unto thee, which deliverest the poor from him that is too strong for him, yea, the poor and the needy from him that spoileth him?" And in Psalms 41: 1 David says, "Blessed is he that considereth the poor: the Lord will deliver him in time of trouble. 2. The Lord will protect him and keep him alive: and he shall be blessed upon the earth; and thou wilt not deliver him unto the will of his enemies." This world has a tendency to praise or lift up those that are more fortunate than some. But Jesus doesn't do that. He lifts up the poor. He cares deeply for the poor. He cares about the outcasts, those that are rejected. Jesus has a heart for hurting, burdened people, that need him. He has a heart for the lost. in Luke 15:4 Jesus says, "What man of you, having a hundred sheep, if he loses one of them, doth not leave the ninety and nine in the wilderness, and go after that which is lost, until he finds it." Jesus would leave the ninety and nine to go find that one little lost lamb.

"He Carries Me"

Once I was a little lamb, lying in a pasture.
I thought it was the end for me, for sure!

I was lying there all helpless, broken as I could be.
But my Shepherd never forgot me.

He was looking everywhere and he left the ninety-nine.
'til he had me taken care of 'til I was doing fine.

He said I was his little one I'll never let you go.
He said, "Little one you're mine, Oh! Don't you know!"

Then he picked me up and carried me, in his strong arms
Now I'm cozy now and resting, free from all alarms.

Peaceful now as I can be.
For I know my Shepherd gently carries me.

I want him to always carry me,
I don't ever want to leave my Shepherd's side.
I want to lay my head on my Shepherd's breast and always abide.

For only he knows the way that I should go.
For only he can direct me, the right path he will show.
For he is my Shepherd I shall not want, he loves me this I know.

For I was just a little one searching for the way.
Then my shepherd came, and picked me up now he carries me today.

The Lord is my Shepherd Oh! He takes good care of me.
Oh! If it wasn't for my Shepherd this little lamb would no longer be.

The Lord is my Shepherd I shall not want he takes care of all my needs.
The Lord is my Shepherd I shall not want.
He lies me down in the pasture, and me he feeds.

The Lord is my Shepherd, I shall thirst no more.
The Lord is my Shepherd, to the sheepfold, he's the Door.

Jesus has a heart for sinners! His heart burns and longs for the lost sheep out of the fold. And he urgently tries to bring them in. Jesus says in John 10:11, I am the Good Shepherd: the good shepherd giveth his life for the sheep." In v.14 Jesus says, "I am the Good Shepherd and know my sheep, and am known of mine. 15. As the Father knoweth me, even so know I the Father; and I lay down my life for the sheep. 16. And other sheep I have which are not of this fold; them also I must bring, and they shall hear my voice; and there shall be one fold, and one Shepherd." Jesus says he is the good shepherd and knows his sheep and they know him. Do you know him as your Shepherd? Has he come and picked you up? Does he lead you everyday? Do you talk with him every day? Knowing Jesus is not "Religion", it is "Relationship". It is both talking and listening. It is giving and receiving. It is bearing one another's burdens. And did you know Jesus has a burden. Yes, he has a burden for the lost. And when you are committed to someone you should share their burden. Jesus is asking us will we share his burden?

"Share My Burden"

I was talking with my Lord,
one peaceful day.
He said you know, my friend,
there is something with you, I need to say.

I have such a burden
for these that are lost.
will you please, my friend
share my burden, no matter the cost?

For I need you to intercede
for you to stand in the gap.
Yes I need you.
Yes you I'm calling, this is no mishap.

For you to share my burden.
For those lost in the clutches of sin.

Will you take the time
to come to me in prayer,
for all of the hurting
the hopeless that is everywhere?

Will you my friend share my burden,
and have eternal blessings unfold?
Or will you care more about
your silver and your gold?

For you see
I'm not looking for ability.
I'm looking for
your availability.

For if you are willing
I'll give you everything you need,
to share my burden.
If you simply say, yes Lord,
use me, I'll Intercede!

Oh! will you give him your burdens and share his? Instead of being burdened with the cares of this life, Jesus will take those cares of this life and give you his burden for lost souls. He'll help you see that the cares of this life are temporary, and he'll help you see your purpose on this earth for eternity. He will give you hope and something to look forward to. He has a work for you to do. You don't have to waste your life anymore living in the past. Jesus has put goals and dreams in your heart. Answer his call now and say yes to him.

"Don't Take Them to the Grave"

Many have died with goals and dreams,
still in their heart.
Words of wisdom,
songs of life, to no-one did they impart.

They tucked them deep
within their soul, never to share.
Their dreams are in the grave today.
Can't take them anywhere.

Oh! Don't hide your dreams
Don't live in Fear, share them with the world.
We need them now to change the lives
of every man, woman, boy and girl.

God has called you now and given you
goals and dreams for you to do.
Get up and follow Jesus
His call on your life to now pursue.

Now is the time
while there is still today.
Step out in Faith
and watch, your God, for you make a way.

You may not have tomorrow,
don't let this time pass.
For tomorrow may not come,
today could be your last.

God has put each and everyone of us here for a reason. You are not here by accident. It doesn't matter if you may have been born illegitimate. God knew your name while you were yet in your Momma's womb. He knew you were going to be here at such a time as this, As Jesus came here on this earth for a purpose. We are here for a purpose. We each one need to find out what our purpose is individually and fulfill it. Jesus says in John 9:4 "I must work the works of him that sent me, while it is day: the night cometh, when no man can work." We must fulfill our calling before it is too late. For night is coming. We must work while it is yet day. For sun down is coming.

"Sun Down is Coming!"

Oh! Father help us labor
while it is yet day.
For the night cometh.
For all the lost help us pray.

For Lord you see the masses
that need your tender Love.
Fill us with compassion
for Heaven is watching from above.

Sun down is coming
Oh! It's almost here
Day will be over
nightfall is near.

Let us work
for the master bringing in the lost.
Bringing them to Jesus
No matter the cost.

Don't make excuses
God will make a way.
He will give you all you need
so work while it is day.

Take a step of faith
out into the deep
For there is a Harvest
for you to reap.

Before Jesus returns hear the Father say
to work hard for him and to labor.
For every thing is ready
He is even at the Door.

Jesus says in John 4:34, "My meat is to do the will of him that sent me, and to finish his work. 35. Say not ye, There are yet four months, and then cometh harvest? Behold, I say unto you, Lift up your eyes and look on the fields; for they are white already to harvest." Jesus said his meat was to do the will of his Father. His meat was to fulfill his purpose on this earth. Jesus kept so focused on the goal, of the plan of the Father and that to him was more important than even eating at times. Jesus walked in the power of the moment. He lived for Eternity. He stayed focused on eternity while living on this earth. He did not get sidetracked with this temporary life. Oh! How easy it is for us to get sidetracked and get our minds and hearts on temporary things without even realizing it. You may be thinking very confidently, "Well, I don't do that. I believe in God. I don't care anything about what this world has to offer." But we need to evaluate and consider our ways. In God's word in the book of Haggai 1:3 God says, "Then came the Word of the Lord by Haggai the prophet, saying 4. Is it time for you, 0 ye to dwell in your roofed houses, and this house lie waste? Now therefore thus saith the Lord of Hosts; Consider your ways, Ye have sown much and bring in little; ye eat, but ye have not enough; ye drink, but ye are not filled with drink; ye clothe ye, but there is none warm; and he that earneth wages, to put it into a bag of holes. Thus saith the Lord of Hosts; consider your ways. 8. Go up to the mountain, and bring wood, and build the house; and I will take pleasure in it, and I will be glorified saith the Lord." We need to consider our ways if all we are concerned about is "our houses, cars and our families". God tells us if we take care of his House first, he would take care of ours. Jesus says in Matthew 6:33, "But seek ye first the kingdom of God and his righteousness and all these things shall be added unto you." We want hope and joy but are we willing to sacrifice and to do what it takes to go after it? It all boils down to how hungry are we for God? We want God and his blessings but are we willing to sacrifice? He gave his all for you and me in hopes in turn we would do the same. In Luke 14 Jesus tells a story of a certain man who made a great supper and invited many. In v. 16 he says, "Then said he unto him, a certain man made a great supper, and invited many. 17. And sent his servant at supper time to say to them that were invited, Come, for all things are now ready. 18. And they all with one consent began to make excuse. The first said unto him, I have bought a piece of ground, and I must needs go and see it; I pray thee have me excused. 19. And another said, I have bought five yoke of oxen, and I go to test them; I pray thee have me excused. 20. And another said, I have married a wife, and therefore I cannot come. 21. So that servant came, and showed his lord these things. Then the master of the house being angry said to his servant, Go out quickly into the streets and lanes of the city and bring in hither the poor, and the maimed and the halt, and the blind." Oh! We all want to be fed. To eat at God's table but we have to stop, get rid of the excuses and make the time. You have to get rid of the distractions and go when the Lord says, Come. And sit down at God's table and let him feed you. You have to make the time. When Moses heard the call from God. He was on the backside of the desert. He was tending to the flock of his father-in-law, Jethro. The Lord appeared to him in the midst of a burning bush, (the Lord can appear to us anyway and any how he wants to). The bush kept burning and did not consume. It just kept burning and burning and burning. So Moses had to stop to see what was going on. So he found someone to tend the sheep and he turned aside to see what was going on. And the Lord seen that he turned around. And Moses went up to the Mountain and the Lord talked with him there. Moses had to work just like we do. He had a family like some of us do. But Moses still took the time out for God. Of Course it was all God in the first place. For God was drawing him. He was calling him to a specific task. Maybe you are dissatisfied and unhappy with where you are at. You may see that "burning bush". And you are in awe of why it isn't consumed. Well! Stop and take time out for God. He wants to speak with you.

"Take Time"

Take time to behold
the beauty of his face.
Take Time to behold
the awesomeness of his Grace.

Take Time to share with Jesus
all of your cares.
For if you Don't Take Time.
Time will
Take you Unawares!

We blame God and get angry with him if things are not going right. And we say God just doesn't do what he says he's going to do. But really we are the ones who have not done anything for Him. He, however, has done everything for us. And we do not deserve it at all. However, we do deserve Hell. But thanks to Jesus, we do not have to get what we deserve. Praise God! When we think of who he is and what he has done for each and everyone of us, he deserves our all. He deserves to be first in our lives. First above our children, our parents, and our own lives. In Luke 14: 26 "Jesus was talking to the great multitude that followed him, for there were a lot of people going after him, but he turned to them and said! If any man come to me, and hate not his father, and mother, and wife, and children, and brethren and sisters, yea, and his own life also, he cannot be my disciple. And whosoever doth not bear his cross, cannot be my disciple. "We have to sacrifice and count the cost. We have to bear our own burdens. We give our burdens to the Lord, but we can't expect anyone else to take responsibility for our own hearts. We can't expect anyone to go get peace, hope, joy and wholeness and salvation for us! We individually have to go receive for ourselves. We individually have to choose to follow Jesus and put him first. In God's word in John 5, there is a story about a man who could not walk for thirty-eight years. He laid around this certain pool called, "Bethesda". Along with a great multitude of impotent folk. Once every season an Angel came down and troubled the water, and whosoever stepped in to the water, was made whole of whatsoever disease he had." Jesus saw this one man who had been cripple thirty-eight years, and he asks him, "wilt thou be made whole?" Then the impotent man began to make excuses; saying he had no one to help put him in the water when it was troubled. He said someone else always beat him in first. Then Jesus saith unto him, "Rise, take up thy bed and walk." v.9 And immediately the man was made whole." Are you spiritually right now like that man? Are you lying there waiting on somebody to give a hand to put you in the water. You can't wait on anyone else to help you. It has got to be between Jesus and you. And he is telling you to "Rise, take up thy bed and walk." Whatever is hindering you from walking with Jesus it has to go now in the name of Jesus! Jesus says in Luke 14:33 "So likewise, whosoever he be of you that forsaketh not all that he hath, he cannot be my disciple." Jesus is calling you to a greater level of commitment. You cannot stay where you are and go with God. When Jesus comes in to our lives and we want to keep our relationship with him alive, we have to move with him. We have to follow him when he tells us too. It is up to us to Listen, Obey and Trust him. When God delivered the Israelites out of Egypt, out of bondage, they had to move "with" God. God would have moved on without them. They had to quickly obey. In Exodus 13:21 God says, "The Lord led them by day in a pillar of a cloud. And by night in a pillar of fire. He took not away the pillar of the cloud by day, nor the pillar of fire by night, from before the people." What an awesome thing that was! But now God has given us an awesome way to lead and guide us. In John 16: 7 Jesus says, "Nevertheless I tell you the truth; It is expedient for you that I go away; for if I go not away, the 'Comforter will not come unto you; but if I depart, I will send him unto you. And when he is come, he will reprove the world of sin, and of righteousness, and of judgment; of sin, because they believe not on me of righteousness, because I go to my Father, and ye see me no more. Of judgment because the prince of this world is judged. I have yet many things to say unto you, but ye cannot grasp them now. 13. Howbeit when he the Spirit of Truth is come, he will guide you into all truth; for he shall not speak of himself; but whatsoever he shall hear, that shall he speak, and he will show you things to come." We don't have to follow a cloud by day or fire by night. Or any other signs. We have right now all we need to lead and guide us. And that is Holy Spirit himself! You don't have to go anywhere else to find peace and happiness. You don't have to go try to drink your problems away. All you need is to know that Holy Spirit is there to be your helper. After Jesus arose from the dead he entered the room where the disciples were. Jesus says in John 21:21, "Peace be unto you; as my Father hath sent me, even so send I you. And when he had said this, he breathed on them, and saith unto them, "Receive ye the Holy Ghost: Whosoever sins ye remit, they are remitted unto them; and whose soever sins ye retain, they are retained." Jesus says in Matthew 28:18-20, "And Jesus came and spake unto them saying, "All Power is given un to me in heaven and in earth. Go ye therefore and teach all nations, baptizing them in the name of the Father, and of the Son, and of the Holy Ghost: Teaching them to observe all things whatsoever I have commanded you. And 20, Lo I am with you alway, even unto the end of the world. Amen. People may say, "Well, I believe in God, isn't that enough?" James says in James 2: 19, "Thou believest that there is one God; thou doest well; the devils also believe and tremble. 20. But wilt thou know 0 vain man that faith without works is dead?" We have to believe and receive Jesus by faith. And believe and receive his Holy Spirit. You may say I believe in Jesus so didn't I receive the Holy Spirit also when I received Jesus? In Acts 2:38 it reads, "Then Peter said unto them, Repent and be baptized everyone of you in the name of Jesus Christ for the remission of sins, and ye shall receive the gift of the Holy Ghost. 39. For the promise is unto you, and to your children, and to all that are afar off, even as many as the Lord our God shall call." God promises us the gift of the Holy Ghost. He is for us and for our children and them that are afar off. Our children do not need to see religion. They don't need any more rules and regulations. What they need is to see Grandpa, Grandma, Dad and Mom walking in the power of the Holy Ghost. What they need is to see the generation before them yielded to the Holy Ghost. We don't need any more counseling sessions or drugs to calm us or our children down. What we need is to yield to the Holy Ghost and let him take complete control. Say this poem as a prayer and mean it with your heart, and I believe the Holy Ghost will come in and transform your life.

"Hold Me Holy Spirit!"

Hold me Holy Spirit
in the cradle of your love.
Comfort me and guide me,
Oh! Heavenly Dove.

I need you to take me,
to lead me, be my guide.
Take over my life completely.
Let me in your arms forever abide.

Thank you for the joy,
of knowing with you I am sealed.
Thank you Holy Spirit, for your power
in my life being revealed.

You've changed my life completely.
I'm forever grateful you have turned me around.
You've taken me off the road to Hell,
and now I'm Heaven bound!

When you receive Jesus with his anointing, for he is the "Anointed One". The Holy Ghost will teach you everything you need to know to help you grow. 1 John 2: 25-27 says, "And this is the promise that he hath promised us, even eternal life. These things have I written unto you, concerning them that 'seduce (deceive) you. 27. But the anointing which ye have received of him abideth in you, and ye need not that any man teach you; but as the same anointing teacheth you of all things and is truth, and is no lie, and even as it hath taught you, ye shall abide in him." Jesus said there will be people that do not know Jesus who Satan uses to deceive you. Jesus says in the last days, many deceivers will come. He says there will be many false prophets. In 1 John 2: 18 God says, "Little children, it is the last time; and as ye have heard that anti-christ shall come, even now are there many anti-christs; whereby we 'know (realize) it is the last time. And in v.20 God says, "But ye have an 'unction (anointing) from the Holy One, and ye know all things." Even when Satan comes with all his little imps to confuse and torment your soul. All you need is Jesus and the Power of the Holy Ghost to make Satan flee. The Holy Ghost will strengthen you and also lead you into all truth. When you rely on him, he will help you and keep you from being deceived. Do you feel like you are so frail, so weak and so small? It's like this world is spinning so fast, and it's so big, and you're so small. And it's like you are screaming just to get off. I don't know how many times I have said that. I was feeling so overwhelmed with all of the things I had to do. I had to go to work, help my kids get ready for school, make their lunch, pay the bills and be concerned with what we were going to have for supper that evening, and it hadn't even came yet. It seemed like everything was just piling up on me. And the clock kept ticking and ticking. I said to my Lord Jesus, Please stop this world. I want to get off, I was serious at the time. I wanted off this ride now! And I was telling my Lord that I didn't ask to be here. Yes, I know my attitude was not right at the time. But my Lord did lovingly remind me, I was here for a reason and when it is my time to go home I will go home. But for now he has me down here to lift his name up, preach his word and lead others to him. Yes, I have repented of an ungrateful attitude. Even though I am longing for home, I am thankful to be here for such a time as this.

"A Little Speck in a Huge World."

Sometimes I feel like such a little speck,
in such a huge, huge world.
It seems like constantly
Satan's fiery darts, to me are hurled.

There's so much that needs
to be done.
So much work to do,
for God's own Son.

Sometimes I feel so small
in my own eyes.
Then Jesus tells me
the day of small things do not despise.

He tells me to go in this thy might,
and I will conquer every enemy.
He tells me I'll win the battle,
if on Him, I rely only.

He'll set me free, no matter how small,
compared to this world I seem.
Greater is He that is in me,
and me he did redeem.

Jesus tells me, "Don't look
at how big the world is.
But tell them one by one,
For them to turn and to trust,
in Jesus, God's Son.

He tells me to just Go
into all the world, and the Gospel tell.
That Jesus Christ is Here today.
He is Alive and Well!

Have you ever said, "Lord, Stop this world I want to get off? I have said that and my Lord showed me how ungrateful I was. He helped me realize we have to be thankful of our very breath. When we say that, we don't realize how that grieves the heart of God. Because he sent his only begotten son Jesus to die on the cross for our sins, and to take our punishment so we could have life and have it more abundantly! God wants us to treasure Life. He paid a tremendous price for us to treasure life.

"Treasure Life"

Don't live your life in drudgery and dread.
Just call on Jesus and by his Spirit be led.

He'll lead you to worship, joy and praise.
He'll make you rejoice, all of your days.

He'll help you see there is
a reason to be, for you and me.

For God has created us for his pleasure.
So don't live in doubt and dread, open life up as a treasure.

There is a reason you are here right now. And it is for such a time as this that we have come into his kingdom. Yes I know things may not be going exactly the way we want them to, but we have Jesus and his Holy Spirit. And we have hope of eternal life. We have eternal life right now. Not just when we leave this world but right now. If you know Jesus, you have eternal life flowing into you right now. Isn't that Awesome? John says in 3:36 "He that believeth on the Son hath everlasting life; and he that believeth not the Son shall not see life; But the wrath of God abideth on him." If we believe right now we have everlasting life and life abundantly. And there is never a dull moment while walking with our Lord.

"Never a Dull Moment"

Never a dull moment
with the Lord by my side.
For he takes me to the mountaintop
through the valley wide.

We're always doing something
while walking here below.
Never a dull moment
when Him I know.

There's never a dull moment
for there's always work to do.
Never a dull moment
for there's a purpose, for me and you.

Never a dull moment
for there's work to be done.
Never a dull moment
while living for Jesus God's Son.

Never a dull moment
when seeking his way and doing his will.
Never a dull moment
when his Spirit, us, he doth fill.

I hear people all the time say, "I am so bored, there is nothing to do. I'm so lonely." And it is so sad, because when walking with Jesus, there is never a boring moment. Mark 16:15-18, Jesus says, "Go ye into all the World, and preach the Gospel to every creature. He that believeth and is baptized shall be saved; but he that believeth not shall be damned. And these signs shall follow them that believe; in my name shall they cast out devils; they shall speak with new tongues; They shall take up serpents; and if they drink any deadly thing, it shall not hurt them; they shall lay hands on the sick, and they shall recover." Jesus says signs shall follow them that believe. I hear people say, "Well, I don't have to speak in tongues, I don't have to do anything to prove I know Jesus." No you don't have to prove anything to anyone. But Jesus says right there, signs shall follow them that believe. What did Jesus do when he walked this earth in the flesh? He lit up this dark world. He tore up the kingdom of darkness. He stormed the Gates of Hell! So no you don't have to do anything. But Jesus is the Same, Yesterday, Today and Forever and if he is living in you, he is still:

"Storming the Gates of Hell!"

Yes, Lord,
by your Grace
I'll take a stand
and look the Devil in the face.

Help me hold on
and help me stand.
Help me take hold
of your nail-pierced hand.

Help me stand Lord,
and never fall.
At the Gates of Hell
may I hear your call.

For though there are
demons all around.
help me not fear Lord.
Help me remember I'm Heaven bound.

And though I have to go
right to where they are.
There are more angels with me,
more powerful by far.

Though Satan tries to keep us from getting
souls out of his clutches.
Use me Lord to storm the Gates of Hell.
To deliver bound souls from their crutches.

Help me Lord never lose sight
of the true battle I am in.
To fight for lost souls
Getting them out of the paths of sin.

For that is one thing
Hell cannot stand,
for someone to storm the gates of Hell,
And Lost souls demand.

Help me never forget
that time is fleeting.
We are here today, gone tomorrow.
And soon with you we will be meeting.

Help me tell others if they don't know you
the Devil is their Father to believe it or not.
For they have to know Hell is a real place,
and it's not Kool but Hot!

Help me Lord not be critical
of the sin they are in.
Give me love and compassion
for Love hides a multitude of sin.

Help me Lord stand,
bold and courageous
Holding your hand.
Though the war around us rages.

Help me stand in faith
and storm the gates of Hell!
Confident and sure, your Word
will not return void. It will Prevail!

In Mark 16: 19 he says, "So then after the Lord had spoken unto them, he was received up into Heaven, and sat on the right hand of God. v. 20 And they went forth, and preached everywhere, the Lord working with them confirming the Word with signs following. Amen. The Lord always confirms his Word.

"He is not a Man that should lie"

You may have had people
lie to you all of your life.
Your way may have been filled,
with nothing but strife.

Well! I know a man
who won't ever lie to you.
What he has promised
that he will do.

Every good and perfect gift,
is from our Heavenly Father above.
Coming down to us
out of his heart full of love.

There is no variableness,
nor shadow of turning.
I can trust this wonderful man
I am learning.

He is faithful and he is kind.
And he honors his Holy Word.
This man is Jesus,
sweet Jesus, my precious Lord.

God honors His Word. When he says he is going to do something he does it. In John 14:1-6, Jesus says, "Let not your heart be troubled; ye believe in God believe also in me. In my Father's House are many mansions; if it were not so, I would have told you. I go to prepare a place for you. And if I go and prepare a place for you, I will come again, and receive you unto myself; that where I am, there ye may be also." Jesus is good on his word. And one thing he has promised us in his word was he was coming back for those of us who love him and are watching for him. And he is going to take us to a place prepared for us.

"Love Letter From Jesus"

Hello,
I'm working hard up here in Heaven.
I'm not sitting passively by.
There's work going on building mansions
up here in the sky.

Just wanted to write and tell you,
what's been going on.
While I'm on my journey.
While I am gone.

There is singing and praising.
And much preparation
for the marriage supper of the Lamb.
I'm coming quickly.
Rest assured, I'm good on my Word.
When I say I'm coming, I am!

Our Father is so anticipating
when he brings all of you children home.
So the day is coming very, very soon
so be ready.
I don't know the day or hour,
it could be at night or at noon.

Just be watching and waiting,
and looking for me in the sky.
For my coming is soon to be.
It is very, very nigh.

There's a lot of work going on up here.
And lot's of work down there below.
The Holy Spirit is moving all across the land.
That I do know.

To bring in the Harvest
and to help you children grow.
Just yield to him completely let him take over.
And you will be ready to go.

Let him use you to make a difference
while you are there below.
So loved ones we are praying for
will be ready to go also.

And keep faithful to me in the work
that I've called you to do.
And one day soon, I'll look and say
Well Done to you

And one more thing in this letter
I do send.
I will give power to rule all nations
to him that overcometh,
and keepeth my works unto the end.

So remember
be watching, working and waiting.
For I am coming back soon for you my friend.
I'll be seeing you very soon
face to face in the end.

sincerely,
Jesus

Jesus is not sitting passively by. He is in Heaven interceding for us all. He is preparing for us a place. And he has given us his Holy Spirit to help us be ready to meet him. Revelation 19:6 says, "And I heard as it were the voice of a great multitude, and as the voice of many waters, and as the voice of mighty thunderings saying, Alleluia; for the Lord God omnipotent reigneth. Let us be glad and rejoice, and give honor, to him; for the marriage of the Lamb is come, and his wife hath made herself ready. And to her was granted that she should be dressed in fine linen, clean and white; for the fine linen is the righteousness of Saints. And he saith unto me, Write, Blessed are they which are called unto the Marriage Supper of the Lamb. And he saith unto me these are the true sayings of God."

Oh! Do you feel
the stirring of something going on?
Oh! The Wedding
of the Bride and Groom
will be here before long.

Hurry be ready,
with your wedding garments on.
The Wedding could start any moment
and the wedding party will be gone.

There is going to be a wedding
soon and very soon.
The Bride will be united
with her loving Groom.

Are you getting ready
getting dressed to attend?
Have you made your reservation
my friend?

The invitation has been sent
to each and everyone.
So make your reservation.
Call on Jesus God's Son.

For soon the Groom will step out
and call his pure, blood washed Bride.
The wedding march will sound
and she'll be by his side.

Are you ready for that Wedding Day
to finally arrive?
Are you living in excitement
the Greatest day to be alive?

Are you living in excitement waiting for that day? Waiting to be reunited to your Groom. Are you looking for Jesus? Eagerly anticipating when you and he meet face to face?

Are You Ready?

Are you ready, Are you ready,
for the Masters call today?
Are you ready, are you ready,
should he call your soul away?
One day soon he's gonna come
and take his bride, to his home.
So be ready for it could be today.

Are you working for the Master
'til the ending of the day?
Doing all you can for Jesus
bringing all to him without delay.

For he's waiting for so many,
that are out there in sin.
To be washed in his blood,
and be born again.

Oh! Be ready for the call
that so many of us wait.
He's going to step out on the Portals

of Heavens Pearly Gates.
He's going to say,
Come home my children
it's getting much too late.

It's time to come home
where you all belong.
You can't stay on Earth.
So lift up your head,
and sing redemptions song!

When you love someone that has went away for a little while and they told you they were just going for a short time and they would return. And when they returned they were going to come back and get you. If you really loved that one and you could not wait to see them you would be looking and expecting everyday, wouldn't you?

"If I Went on a Journey"

If I went on a Journey
and left loved ones behind.
And I told them I'd be back,
please keep it in mind.

I'm going to prepare a place
for you and I to share.
I'm going to be back
to take you over there.

And if I went on a Journey
Oh! Would you forget me.
Or would you be ready
to come and go with me?

I'm coming quickly
in the twinkling of an eye.

I'm coming soon to take you
to our home on High.

If I went on a journey
would you long for me?
Would you long
for my face to see?

Or would you look to others
and forget me you ever knew.
Oh! Tell me if I went on a Journey
what would you do?

For Jesus asks this question to us today.
He's gone on a Journey
but he's coming back.
For with his promises
he is not slack.

He said he was coming back
like a thief in the night.
Today could be the day
so make things right.

For he's coming, he's coming.
Like a thief in the night.
So be ready and watching,
and make things right!

One day soon, nobody knows the day or the hour, but Jesus Christ is going to come back in the clouds, just as he left. In Mark 14:61 says, "The High Priest stood up and asked Jesus, "Art thou the Christ, the son of the Blessed? He asked him that before he went to the cross. And Jesus said in v. 62 I am; and ye shall see the son of man sitting on the right hand of power, and coming in the clouds." Then the High Priest accused him of blasphemy because Jesus told him he was the Son of God. You know one day everyone will see him and those also that pierced him. Revelation 1:7 says, "Behold he cometh with clouds; and every eye shall see him, and they also which pierced him; and all kindreds of the earth shall wail because of him. Even so, Amen." And in Acts 1:9, says "And when he had spoken these things while they watched, he was taken up; and a cloud received him out of their sight. v. 10 And while they looked steadfastly toward heaven as he went up, behold two men stood by them in white apparel; v.11 Which also said, Ye men of Galilee, why stand ye gazing up into heaven? This same Jesus, which is taken up from you into heaven, shall so come in like manner as ye have seen him go into heaven."

"Coming Back in the Clouds"

My child, look up
to the clouds above.
For I'm coming back in them
to receive those who me, do love.

I'm coming back for those
who are watching and waiting
So don't lose heart, look up my child,
and keep anticipating.

For I promised when I left
in the clouds long ago,
That I will return the same way
for those I know.

I could come back at any time.
So please be ready to go.
The time, day or hour
I do not know.

So always be ready
with your garments on.
And your lamps all trimmed and burning
shining like the sun.

For if your lights are shining
burning bright.
You are going to see your way
in this dark night.

And know I can come any time, any day.
So tell others also I'm coming soon again.
To trust in me
and turn from all sin.

I'm coming in the clouds
one day everyone will see.
That I'm faithful and true.
What I've said will come to be!

In a Jewish wedding (if I have this correct), the man asks the woman to marry him and if she says yes, he goes away with his Dad and prepares her a place. And only when it is ready for her, he returns. He leaves her and just tells her he shall return. And it is up to her to take him at his word, and be ready for him.

"I Shall Return!"

One night while talking with my precious Lord,
and reading his Holy Word.

My Lord, gently, says to me, "Though the world you're living in,
is full of chaos and sin.

You're wanting so bad to come home, keep watching for me..
For I'm coming back you will see.

I'm coming back for my Bride.
For I want her by my side.

I'm coming back this could be the day.
I'm coming back come what may.

I'm coming back as a thief in the night.
keep watching and waiting, keep the candle bright.

I'll come back, so you will be with me,
and from this sinful world be free.

So keep watching and waiting for I know not the day or hour.
But just know I am coming in all my Glory and Power.

Tell my people, I am coming, I shall return.
I'm coming back, receive my love don't spurn.

For I'm coming for those who love me,
Everyone will see.

For I will finish this short work upon the earth.
Tell everyone they have to have a second birth.

For then and only then will they go with me.
To Heaven for all Eternity."

In the Jewish relationship, the Bridegroom tells her he will return then leaves to prepare. It is up to the Bride to not forget the bridegroom. She should be always anticipating when they shall meet again. It is up to her to keep the fire burning. It is up to her to keep looking and to stay ready.

"Don't Let The Fire Die!"

Oh! Lord I remember
when we first met.
Oh! What a fire to this heart of mine
you did set.

You came to me when my heart
was dry as a desert.
Full of loneliness, pain
despair and hurt.

I was looking for meaning
and a reason to be.
You were there, and you opened,
my blinded eyes to see.

You came in when in my heart
I panted only for you.
Just as I longed for
my heart you did renew.

Now time has passed since that happy day,
when your eyes and mine had met.
I thank you, Lord for the fire
in my heart you did set.
And Lord I don't want it to ever die.
But only hotter and bigger to get.

I want this fire
in my heart to spread.
To where I am consumed
and by it, I only am led.

Help me never get to used
to you being near.
May my heart always be stirred,
when your sweet voice I hear.

At the thought of you
may my heart pound.
Of you my one and only
always being around.

May my heart melt
when I mention your name.
May my love for you, be as your love for me.
Never changing, always the same.

Jesus says in Matthew 25:1 "Then shall the kingdom of heaven, be likened unto ten virgins, which took their lamps, and went forth to meet the bridegroom. And five of them were wise and five were foolish. v.3 They that were foolish took their lamps and took no oil with them: v. 4 But the wise took oil in their vessels with their lamps. The wise made sure they were ready. They took oil for their vessels.

"Go Bring Those Vessels To Me"

Look around you and see, all the needs in this world.
We have to tell them now of Jesus' love unfurled.
Time is running out.Oh! Can't you see?
Jesus wants to use you. He says, "Go bring those vessels to me.
Don't just think of yourself for I've already set you free.
You must go now, and tell them, what is coming to be.
And tell them now, that I died for their sin.
But I arose from the dead, and I'm coming soon again.
See right now they have this chance, to call upon my name.
Tell them that you're saved, and for them I've done the same.
Tell them I could come right this very hour.
Tell them if they just ask me, I'd give them the power.
Bring them all, bring them all, bring all the vessels to me.
Bring them all, bring them all, bring the vessels to me.
Bring them all, bring them all the broken and the marred
Bring them all, bring them all, the bruised and the scarred.
The trumpet is going to sound, their lamps must be all trimmed and burning.
Oh! Hear my heart hear my pleadings, Oh! Hear my constant yearning!
Oh! My people hear my heart.
I don't want any of us to have to part!

They've just got to know just how very much I love them so.
So please, please Go
Bring those vessels to me.
So we can all be together in Eternity.

Paul says in Colossians 4: 5 "Walk in Wisdom toward them that are without, redeeming the time." The wise virgins did what it took to stay ready. They took their bridegroom seriously! They lived for their grooms' return. Are you living for Jesus' return? Jesus is our bridegroom and he is reminding his bride to watch for he is coming soon.

"Watch For Me"

I'm coming back for you.
So don't be troubled
I've gone to prepare a special place for you.
So where I am there you may be too.
So be ready I'm coming back for you.

Please don't get tired
of waiting for me.
Just hang on,
I'll be back, you will see.

I know it's hard
for you to wait.
But don't get discouraged
I'll not be late.

Hang on to Hope
and don't let it go.
Hold fast my bride
to what you know.

I'll be back when it's time
So just keep looking up
to the Eastern sky.
And my bride, hold your head up high.

Don't let anyone or anything
get you down.
For I haven't left you hopeless,
there's no need to frown.

The trials you have
are only for a short while.
So keep yourself my bride
free from all sin, and free from all guile.

Don't let the trials take the hope
that you have in your heart.
No matter what happens while you are there below.
With Heaven you are a part!

So Rejoice, Rejoice
The best is yet to come.
For I will soon return and take you
to our Beautiful, Heavenly Home!

In Matthew 25:5 Jesus says, "While the Bridegroom tarried, they all slumbered and slept. And those were the ones left behind. It all boils down to how much we love our Lord Jesus! How bad do we want to be with him? How bad do we want to be ready?

"No Time For Resting"

There is no time for resting.
This is time for War.
We can't slumber and sleep,
and our Jesus ignore.

For Satan and his demons bands
are trying to take control.
We can't sit back and let him do it.
We can't let him have not one breathing soul.

The time is drawing nigh
for Jesus' return.
Many are still living in sin.
And many are going to burn.

We have to keep our eyes on Jesus
but also look around.
We have to go tell them and
proclaim the Gospel sound.

There's no time for resting
in this battle that we're in.
We've got to warn sinners
of the consequences of sin.

We've got to bring them
over to our side.
For if they turn to Jesus
they will not be denied!

We have got to be on guard against falling asleep spiritually. We have got to stay sober and awake in this world, and keep our hearts and minds focused on Eternity. We have to get up and get ready. We all have an appointment to make!

"Wake Up! Wake Up!"

Wake up! Wake Up!
The enemy is around.
He's quiet as a mouse
he may not even make a sound.

He's subtle and sly,
as a sly old fox.
He's stealing your goods, as you sleep,
and the clock tick tocks.

Arise! Arise!
everything may look okay.
And may be pleasing to the eyes.
But don't get hooked,
it's an enemy in disguise.

Arise! Arise!
There's an enemy behind,
sneaking up by surprise.
Trying to steal your goods,
Don't be foolish, be wise.

Wake Up! Wake Up!
And be sober,
for our Lord's coming is nigh.
Don't sleep, be watching,
for he's coming in the sky.

Satan wants us to forget all about Jesus. He wants us to forget that he came and died for our sins. He wants us to forget that Jesus rose again and is seated at the right hand of the Father interceding for us right now in Heaven. And he also wants us to forget that he is coming back to get those who love him. And take us back to Heaven to be with him. Satan would love for us to get comfortable in this world and forget that we are only passing through. This world is not our final destination. It is either Heaven or Hell. The enemy of our souls wants us to forget that it is the Lord Jesus Christ who gives us everything we have. I have heard that prosperity is a greater test than poverty. I don't know yet, but I would like to find out. Jesus doesn't want us to forget him when he does bless us with prosperity. He said for us not to forget him or the poor when he brings us into our promised land. To always remember where we came from and not forget him.

"Don't Forget Me Saith The Lord"

Over and over I've told you
when you come into the Land I've promised.
Don't forget who took you there.
For you didn't get there on your own.
It was I and my Glory I won't share.

Over and over I'd try to tell you, don't forget me
when you have all the wealth you need.
For it was I, that raised you up.
Out of nothing but a tiny, little seed.

Over and over I've told you don't forget me.
When you're full and satisfied.
It was I, along the way right by your side.

It was not the work of your own hand.
For it was I that brought you
into your Promised Land.

Over and over I'd tell you don't forget me
when your houses are blest.
For I've blest you to be part of your family.
Not just a one time guest.

I've sat back and watched,
and waited on you to put me first.
You didn't need me in the good times.
But only in the worst.

Over and over I've tried to talk to you.
For I've longed for your Love.

I've tried to remind you,
I'm right here with you.
I'm not just "the God above".

It was I who made things work out.
It was I who opened doors for you.
in my Love and Mercy,
I'd gently whisper which one to walk through.

But what has happened
to the closeness we once did share?
You've left it all behind.
in your hopes to get "somewhere".

For I know you've had your plans,
your purposes, your will.
No time anymore with me to be still.

For you have no time, no need, no desire,
for me any longer.
Do you think maybe,
without me you are stronger?

Well! I guess
that is your thoughts for your actions are quite clear.
For you would do things different,
you'd go out of your way, to show me to stay near.

Well! I guess, everything is going well.
Everything is okay, you don't want me anymore.
Well! Goodbye. I'll be moving on.
I'm going now, I'm out the door!

I'm gone my Love.
Do you miss me yet?
You didn't even answer.
You don't even know I'm gone.

I guess without me, your life is set.

Well! Go ahead.
Enjoy your life of so-called comfort and ease.
Live your life without me.
Just as you please.

But if you won't let me in your Earthly home.
And you keep thinking everything is Fine.
How can you expect
When your Earthly life is over
that I can let you into mine?

For I am the Way, the Truth and the Life.
And to Heaven I am the Only Door.
If you choose to forget me, we will be apart.
Forever and Ever More!

If you don't let me in your Earthly Tabernacle,
and on earth you don't let me inside.
How can you expect
a home in Heaven to Abide?

If you keep choosing to tell me
to let you be,
don't you know we will be apart
for all Eternity?

And know this if you forget me
and your heart continues to roam
you won't hear the call from Heaven
when the Father calls you home.

So please my Love
no longer take my love for granted.
For I Love You!
Don't forget me.
And I promise I will remember you,
when your Earthly Life is Through!

Jesus says in Matthew 24: 42, "Watch therefore: for ye know not what hour your Lord doth come. But know this that if the goodman of the house had known in what watch the thief would come, he would have watched, and would not have suffered his house to be broken into. Therefore be ye also ready; for in such an hour as ye think not the Son of Man cometh. Who then is a faithful and wise servant, whom his Lord hath made ruler over his household, to give them meat in due season? Blessed is that servant whom his Lord when he cometh shall find so doing, verily I say unto you, that he shall make him ruler over all his goods." Satan the enemy of our souls tries whatever he can to lull us to sleep. We have to keep our eyes on Jesus so we won't fall asleep in all this darkness.

"Keep Me Awake"

Lord, I need your light
to shine on me.
For this world is so dark
Oh! Lord I cannot see.

Take away the darkness
so I can find my way.
Lord I'm tired and weary.
Shine your light I pray.

There's darkness everywhere

trying to block my view.
Oh! Lord shine your light.
For I need you.

Sometimes all this darkness,
makes me just want to sleep.
Wake me up with your light,
my soul please keep.

Keep me awake, in all this darkness,
that surrounds my soul.
Oh! Lord Don't let me sleep.
Don't let the darkness take control.

Lord I'm trying so hard
in all this darkness to stay awake.
Keep me awake in Your Light,
for Heavens' sake.

You know it is all a matter of love, passion and desire. What do we Love? Or shall I say Who do we Love? If we love Jesus we will walk in his light. If we love Jesus we will want to spend time with him. We will want to be where he is at. We will long for him and desire to please him. If we really believe Jesus is coming back for those who love him, we will definitely be determined to be ready because we love him. No matter how long it takes, waiting will not even be a problem. I know it gets hard sometimes to wait, but you know you are waiting for an awesome reason. You know your waiting is definitely worthwhile. 2 Peter 3: 3 says, "Knowing this first that there shall come in the last days scoffers, walking after their own lusts, and saying, "Where is the promise of his coming: For since the fathers fell asleep, all things continue as they were from the beginning of creation." God says in the last days there will be people saying, "Where is the promise of his coming?" There will be people saying I have heard that Jesus was coming all of my life and he hasn't came yet. I hope if you are reading this that you are not one of those people. Or maybe you are one of those people and you are now changing your way of thinking. Maybe now you are waking up and instead of being a scoffer, now you are seriously waiting on our Lord Jesus' return.

"Keep Waiting He Will Come"

Sometimes it may seem that our Lord comes much too late.
I know it's hard sometimes on him to wait.

But hang on, he won't let you down.
He's a good God, who knows what he is doing, I have found.

His ways are not our ways, his thoughts are higher than ours.
So just wait on him no matter the days, no matter the hours.

He does things on his time, this we must know.
He'll answer when to him we go.

He won't cast us out.
Just keep believing and cast away all doubt.

Jesus will not fail us, no matter how bad it may seem.
For that is why he came for us to redeem.

The God I know is faithful, he cannot tell a lie.
He keeps promises, so don't just sit around and sigh.

Get up and rejoice, and Praise the Lord.
For Jesus will come, he honors his Word!

And at midnight there was a cry made, Behold the Bridegroom cometh; go ye out to meet him. Matthew 25:6. I have heard if that is correct that the call that the bridegroom is coming is right before the bridegroom is there. The house is completed and it is time. For us, the call of the "Bridegroom" coming has been sounding off already. We have to be up and ready. There isn't much time left now. Isaiah says in Isaiah 60:1,2 "Arise, shine; for thy light is come, and the glory of the Lord is risen upon thee. 2. For, behold, the darkness shall cover the earth, and gross darkness the people; but the Lord shall arise upon thee, and his glory shall be seen upon thee."

"Arise"

Get up and arise.
For our Lord is coming
in the skies.
To take away his own,
he is coming for the wise.
Who is watching and ready
to leave this world of lies.
So get up and arise.
Wipe the sleep out of your eyes.
Everyone shall see him
when he comes in the clouds.
Himself he'll not disguise.
So talk to him and pray
commit your life today,
so you he will recognize.

Matthew 25:7 says "Then all those virgins arose, and trimmed their lamps. And the foolish said unto the wise, give us of your oil; for our lamps are gone out. But the wise answered saying, Not so; lest there be not enough for us and you; but go ye rather to them that sell, and buy for yourselves and while they went to buy the bridegroom came; and they that were ready went in with him to the marriage; and the door was shut. Afterward came also the other virgins, saying, Lord, Lord open to us, but he answered and said, Verily I say unto you, I do not recognize you." There is going to be people who think they will go to Heaven just because of an experience of some kind they have had ten, twenty, thirty, forty or even fifty years ago. We can't go by what happened years and years ago. Now don't get me wrong I am not diminishing the fact that something did happen if it did. But what I am saying is those wise virgins in that parable that Jesus was talking about, they kept oil in their lamps, for the Bridegroom. They stayed ready. They kept a fresh attitude concerning their bridegroom even though he was not physically there. They trusted him to return. How long has it been since you really talked with the Lord? And really poured out your heart to him, and really, really listened to him in return?

"How Long Has It Been?"

How long has it been
since you bowed your knee in prayer?
To talk with the Lord
and all your problems share.

How long has it been
since you've asked the Lord,
to cleanse you from all sin?
Oh! How long has it been?

How long has it been since you
got alone with him.
And told him all
of your troubles that you were in?

How long has it been since you
showed him your love?
He died for your sins.
He's shown you enough.

He daily loads you
with blessings from above.
Oh! How long has it been
since you've shown him your love?

How long has it been since you

have acknowledged that he's there?
How long has it been since you've
thanked him for his care?

He loved us first
while we were dying in our sin.
How long since you've thanked him?
Oh! How long has it been?

Please don't be one of those that the Lord looks at and says "I do not recognize you". Or "Depart from me I never knew you!" It is one thing to know someone by name. And it is quite another thing to really know someone intimately.

"Have You Been With Jesus?"

Out in the cold, dreary night,
you can hear voices out of sight.

There are so many voices in the wind.
So many voices it can send.

I don't want to hear what they say.
I only want one voice to come my way.

That's the voice of my Lord.
I only want to hear his word.

I only want to hear what comes from him.
Anything else might lead to sin.

So before you give me any advice,
If it's not from Jesus, think twice.

If you haven't been with Jesus and talked it out.
You don't know anything without a doubt.

If you haven't been in God's throne room.
What you advise, just might lead to doom.

I don't care if you've been to church yesterday.
What matters most, have you been with Jesus today?

It seems like every time you turn around someone is giving you their opinion. Even when you do not ask for it We have to be very careful with who we listen to and who we take direction from. For if they do not know Jesus and are not seeking the Lord for you they could very well lead you astray. They could lead you down a road where the end is utter destruction. It may appear all well and good at the beginning but subtly lead you to spiritual death. I was over at my Mother's house the other day and she had a well known talk show on the television at the time. This particular program there was some "Psychic" woman on there supposedly answering peoples' questions about their lives and the lives of their loved ones. I flipped the channel. And you know it is so sad. Because there is hope without having to talk to some so called psychic. And we better know the truth of God's word. Jesus will tell us everything we need to know. And if he doesn't tell us maybe we don't need to know in the first place. The point is Jesus is the Answer! Jesus Christ will light our way if we are in darkness and cannot find our way. We don't need any psychic. And I am going to say this and I don't care who doesn't like it. We don't need a Psychiatrist. And we don't need more pills. All we need is Jesus, Jesus, Jesus. And Holy Spirit is our Counselor, our Psychiatrist! And also as the word of God says in Proverbs 3:4-6 "Trust in the Lord with all of your heart and lean not unto your own understanding. And in all thy ways acknowledge him and he shall direct your paths. "

You know we all want Hope, Love, Joy, Peace, Happiness and Contentment. And we would be lying if we said we didn't. Jesus Christ offers it to us. And all we have to do is accept, believe and confess. John says in Revelation 12: 11 "And they overcame him by the blood of the Lamb, and by the word of their testimony; and they loved not their lives unto the death." When we yield our lives to Jesus and receive his precious Holy Spirit we have Life! When we give our lives to Jesus we step out of Darkness and into God's marvelous light. We're no longer empty. When we allow Jesus to come in we are filled with Hope, Life, Peace and Joy. Paul says in Romans 14:17 the kingdom of God is not eating and drinking; But righteousness and peace and joy, in the Holy Ghost. For he that in these things serveth Christ is acceptable to God, and approved of men. Let us therefore follow after the things which make for peace. And things wherewith one may build up another." Jesus wants us to serve, love and obey him out of love. It is not a burden to listen to the Lord and obey him. It is a blessing and it is an honor. He is a good God. And he loves us so much. It is for our good when we obey him. How would we like it if our spouse, children or someone else we loved, acted like it was such a burden and such a grudge to have you around? I've had that happen to me before and it is not a very good feeling. It hurts. Sometimes we need to stop and take a look at how we treat Jesus. How do we talk to him? Do we hog or control all of the conversation? Or do we listen to every word he says? How do we feel when we are walking in the mall or store and the friend you are with runs into another friend and leaves you standing there alone? They don't introduce you at all and they also ignore you. They talk to each other for what seemed like hours. Yes, it probably would hurt. Don't you think? Not that you are a jealous person but it is the fact that you were with them and all of a sudden they forgot you and ignored you. Do you know how it feels when you've waited so long to share something with your loved one only to have them turn a deaf ear or disbelieve you? It really hurts. You know too many times we do that with our Lord without even being aware of it. We walk with other friends without introducing him. We ignore him and act like we don't know him when we are with someone else. We turn a deaf ear when he so wants to share something special with us. Or we disbelieve him when we do listen. Listen closely we might hear Jesus say,

"I Thought You Were My Friend"

I got up today in the usual way.
Went along and forgot to pray.
I was in a hurry running out of time.
Had to get ready for the day.

Now the times gone by,
still haven't had much time to pray.
Met another old friend along the way.
Talked to her mostly half of the day.
My Best Friend, to her, I did not introduce.
I had too much other stuff to say.

Now times gone on,
still hadn't had much time to pray.
Then I heard a voice gently say,
"I thought you were my friend."

I thought you were my friend.
You don't even talk to me at all.
You only want me when you fall.
To have a friend it is a two-way street.
And when at the cross we did meet.
Remember then you were so complete.

Now you have so many other things,
heavy on your mind.
Time for me anymore is very hard to find.
I heard a voice gently say,
"We committed we'll love each other to the end.
Why don't you act
like you are truly my friend?"

Friends will tell their deepest thoughts.
And all their secrets share.
They take the time to love each other,
to show how much they care.

Time went on and I went to bed.
Not one word to my Best Friend (Jesus) I said.
Pulled the covers back
on the pillow I laid my head.
Then I heard a voice gently say,
"I thought you were my friend."

Well, another day for me has dawned.
I got out of bed, stretched and yawned.
Never thought about, my best friend (Jesus).
Who wanted to talk with me.
I heard a voice gently say,
"Talk with me I plea!"
I have so much to tell.
But I guess you think without me, all is well.

I ran on ignoring my friend.
Deadlines to make
bills to send.
I never intended my best friend to forsake.

I had to get ready for the day.
I had many things to my best friend to say.
But time didn't permit.I had to go.
Then I heard a voice gently say,
"How can you claim me you know?"
When your love for me you never show.

Still I went on not saying a word.
To my Best Friend (My Lord).
My life was getting
more and more confused,
and more and more absurd.

I had big decisions to make.
But time to seek my Lord's counsel
I unwisely did not take.

I didn't mean my Lord to forsake.
But here I now am,
full of loneliness and heartache.

Then I heard a voice gently say,
"I hope you are still my friend.
If you are, give me your heart to mend!"

We want joy, peace and love. But we will only get those things when we choose to obey God out of Love. It is not a burden to serve the Lord. It is a Joy, and Honor and a Privilege! An awesome, awesome privilege!

"It's A Privilege to Serve God"

I count it a privilege
to bow my knee in prayer.
Just to know that when I do,
my Heavenly Father is waiting there.

He loves me to share my all with him.
All my Heartache, sorrow and my joy.
For if I go to him, with my cares.
in my heart peace to me, he will employ.

He tells me to come with thanksgiving.
And to him let my requests be known.
He takes delight in hearing from me.
So knowing that, I can go boldly to his throne.

If I had to bear my burdens alone,
I don't know what I'd do.
So I count it an honor to go to him.
For I know he'll see me through.
It's an honor also, to talk to him,
not just when I'm feeling blue.

For when I bow my knee in prayer
I don't find an angry God there.
I find a loving Father who with him
I can communicate.
Yes he's holy and yes he's just,
even so, with my cares he can still relate.

I don't have to be lonely, discouraged or scared.
For his Son Jesus on the cross of Calvary,
all my sins and griefs had bared.

So I can live happy, joyful and free.
Because I have a Heavenly Father who loves me.
Who sent his Son Jesus to set me free.
Thanks to him I can have life
and have it more abundantly.

My Father tells me not to let Satan
rob me of what he's given.
For if I have trusted in Jesus,
eternal life I do have
and in heaven I will be living.

Father God tells me, Satan will lie
and tell you I don't hear.
Satan would love for you
to waste your days in fear.

So that's when I put on
my helmet of salvation.
And look Satan in the eyes,
and tell him, "Look I am in relation

to the Father, Son and Holy Ghost.
Jesus is my shield
Gods' Word is my Sword.
So I start speaking the Word
in the name of the Lord.

I look Satan in the eyes
and tell him It is Written!"
Satan expects me to fear and cower away.
But I quote Gods' Word then Satan is surely smitten.

I tell him I won't waste another day,
listening to his lies.
For Gods' word I choose to believe.
Gods' word my fears it will relieve.

My Heavenly Father reminds me,
when Satan comes against me
tell him Gods' word sets me free!

You say Satan, It is written.
Thou shalt worship the Lord thy God,
and him only shalt thou serve.
So get thee behind!
So if you start doing that
you'll feel much better you'll find.

I won't waste another day
living in fear, unbelief and doubt.
I'm going to rise up and tell everybody,
I Love you Jesus with a shout!

I won't worship you Satan
by grumbling and complaining.
I'm going to worship Jesus, by his Grace.
The rest of my days on this earth remaining.

I won't worship myself
with my selfish pride.
Jesus Christ is Lord of Everything,
in him I will Abide!

Yes we do have an enemy (Satan) who is always trying to steal, kill and destroy us. But we have God's Word, which is more powerful than a two-edged sword. Paul says in the book of Hebrews 4: 12, "For the word of God is quick and powerful, and sharper than any two-edged sword, piercing even to the dividing asunder of soul and spirit, and of the joints and marrow, and is a discerner of the thoughts and intents of the heart." We need to be thankful for the Word of God.

"Oh! Father Thank You For Your Word!"

Oh! Father how I love your Word.
And hold it dear to my Heart.
There's no way from it
I ever want to part.
For it's his Word
that has given me a new start.

It's how with my Heavenly Father
I keep in contact.
Without his Word I would be lost
and that's a fact.

His Word gives Life
to my very being.
It's all because
of His mighty Word I am seeing.

His Word is my food
I feast upon.
For it's My Savior
God's precious Holy Son.

God's Word is my sword
and my shield.
I am blessed when I read and obey.
And to it's truths humbly yield.

It is my light
through the darkest, deepest valley.
Oh! How it comforts
and lights the way for me.

I just wouldn't make it
through this world today.
without God and his word
guiding my way.
It guides my footsteps and gives me strength.
Step by step. Day by day.

My Heavenly Father uses his word
for me and him to communicate.
So read his Word and obey it,
before it's too late.

As David says in Psalms 119 "Thy Word is a lamp unto my feet and a light unto my path." And in John 1:1-5 "In the beginning was the Word, and the Word was with God, and the Word was God. 2. The same was in the beginning with God. 3. All things were made by him; and without him was not any thing made that was made. 4. In him was life; and the life was the light of men. 5. And the light shineth in darkness; and the darkness overpowered it not."

"I'll Be With The Word In Heaven"

Many times while I was reading
Gods' precious Holy Word.
I've dropped countless tears on its pages,
of things I have heard.

One day I'll read for the last time,
the precious Word of God.
I'll need it no more
for in Heaven my feet will be shod.
When I step through deaths' door.

I'll read Gods word no more.
For I'll be with Him in Heaven.
When I go through Deaths' Door.

John 1: 14 says "And the Word was made flesh, and dwelt among us, (and we beheld his glory, the glory as of the only begotten of the Father) full of grace and truth." God's Word was given for us.

"Written For Our Comfort"

Here in the pages
of God's sacred, Holy Word.
Are the greatest words
ever penned, ever heard.

Some don't want to hear it.
Or believe it does exist.
They ignore it or mock it
and push it aside and very often resist.

If they'd only wake up and realize.
It was given for our good
to open our eyes.

To show us how to walk.
To show us how to love.
And show us how to talk.

So take the privilege to read God's Word.
For it was written for our comfort.
That we should have hope.
So receive God's Word with Joy.
So with this earthly life we more than cope.

For without God's Word this world
how void it would be.
For it was his word that made
all things beautiful that we see.

Look how awesome and powerful it is
my, my, my.
His word is there to change our lives.
You will be the next to testify..

You haven't got anything to lose.
But everything to gain.
All you have to do is choose.
So next time you're in pain.

And you're questioning why?
Read God's Word for comfort.
Give Gods' word a try.
For the Author is ever present.
He's the greatest counselor
He will more than satisfy!

We cannot be happy and joyful if we are in disagreement with the Lord. If we are not obeying God's Word we are in disobedience and therefore we will not prosper! His word says his wrath is on the disobedient. We are either walking with Jesus (the Word of God) or we are walking contrary to him. If we are walking with him, obeying his word, we are blessed. If we are not obeying him (the Word) we are cursed.

"Obey God's Word"

Thy Word is a lamp unto me feet, and a light unto my path.
If I be a hearer and a doer I will escape God's wrath.

'Cause one day God is going to judge this world because of sin.
The party will be over so turn from your ways and win.

So read Gods' word and obey it
keep going don't ever quit.

Cling to Jesus real tight.
Obey God's word, turn your darkness into light.

We are only cheating ourselves when we are not a doer of God's Word. James 1:21 says, "Wherefore lay apart all filthiness and superfluity of naughtiness, and receive with meekness the engrafted word, which is able to save your souls." We have to receive God's word and hide it in our heart. For what would happen if it ever came the day when the freedom to read our bibles would be taken away from us? How much of it do you know? How much would the Holy Spirit be able to bring to your remembrance? As David says in Psalm 119: 11, "Thy word have I hid in mine heart, that I might not sin against thee."

"Hide God's Word In Your Heart"

Get God's word in your heart.
And from it's scriptures never part.

For if it ever comes the Day,
when they take our Bibles away.

We'll have it hid deep inside.
So open your hearts and your mouth wide.

And fill it up overflowing
filled with Jesus ever growing.

For they can take it from our home,
but from it's scriptures we'll never roam.

And they can take it from our hand.
And even take it from our Land.

But if we have it hid in our heart,
there's no way from it we can part.

So get God's word and it impart..
Now is time for us to start!

James 1:22 says, "But be ye doers of the Word and not hearers only, cheating your own selves. For if any be a hearer of the Word and not a doer he is like unto a man beholding his natural face in a mirror. For he beholdeth himself and goeth his way and immediately forgetteth what manner of man he was." We can sit and hear the Word of God but if we do not yield to the Word and obey him, we will not be joyful. For joy comes when we obey! Joy comes when we die to self. When we allow Jesus to rule on the throne of our heart instead of our self. When we quit beholding our selves and get into God's Word and obey it. Joy comes when we get into God's presence and Behold Him! We have to get our eyes off of our selves and onto Jesus. Get into his word and obey it. And I don't mean religion. Seek Jesus and then His Word will come alive to you and get in agreement with him. By obeying his word and walking with him. He will not lead you on if you have not obeyed in the last thing he has told you to do. So obey him and be blessed! You will not get anywhere except stuck in a rut and more miserable every day you are disobedient. If you are in a rut right now and feel like you can't get out, call on Jesus, he will lift you out. You may have been disobedient before, and you find yourself so unhappy, so discontent and discouraged. And it may feel like you are just being overwhelmed by all of your problems, stop and repent and get in agreement with what you know the Lord has told you to do. You will be blessed! James 1:25 says, "But whoso looketh into the perfect law of liberty, and continueth therein, he being not a forgetful hearer, but a doer of the work, this man shall be blessed in his deed." See, many people want the Lord with them but they don't want to obey his word. we think our sin tastes good or feels good. we need to taste and see that the Lord is good. People want the Lord but want sin also. Oh! How wretched and miserable we are when we try to straddle the fence! If we want to truly be happy, free and joyful we need to stay off of that fence and stay on the Lords' side. And walk with him Wholly! With all of our heart! Holy! 1 Peter 1:13-16 says, "Wherefore gird up the loins of your mind, be sober and hope to the end for the grace that is to be brought unto you at the revelation of Jesus Christ: 14. As obedient children, not fashioning yourselves according to the former lusts in your ignorance; 15. But as he which hath called you is holy, so be ye holy in all manner of conversation; 16. Because it is written, Be ye Holy; For I am holy."

"The Trumpet is Fixing to Sound"

Oh! Lord help us wake up
and see what's happening all around.
There is wars and rumors of wars.
The trumpet is fixing to sound!

People hurrying all around
doing their own thing.
Jesus wake them up
and to their knees please bring.

For there are famines
earthquakes and pestilences.
And too many people
trying to sit on fences.

Backbiting, hatred, strife,
criticizing and judging people all around.
Oh! Lord wake us up,
the trumpet is fixing to sound.

And Lord does anybody Love
anybody anymore?
Love isn't like
it was once before.

And Lord help us see we either love or hate
there is really no middle ground.
Oh! Lord help us wake up.
The trumpet is fixing to sound.

Thank you Lord for keeping us
safe and secure.
Oh! Help us sweet Jesus
and to the end we'll endure.

Lord you said the love of many shall wax cold,
because sin shall abound.
Oh! Lord wake us up,
The Trumpet is Fixing to Sound!

This is no time for spiritual fence straddling. Jesus Christ will give us the power to overcome when we put our faith in him. We are Overcomers! We are Blood Bought children of the Living God! We are more than conquerors! Now lets get up and be what God has created us to be!

"Overcomer"

I'm an Overcomer in this world below.
Because my Daddy in Heaven told me so.

He said, "Don't go by what you feel.
Go by what I said, in my Word, for it is real.

Don't you look at others along this way.
Child listen to what I have to say.

You have my strength.You have my power.You are mine!
Keep it in mind, this very hour and you'll do fine.

Don't you listen if others scoff.
Just turn your head and walk off.

Don't get mad and get revenge.
Just give it to me. I will avenge.

For I'll take good care of you.
Don't you know I'll see you through

I will defend, no one will hurt what is mine!
For I'm watching all of the time, you don't have to have a sign.

Just trust in what I say.
I'm with you all the way.

I'll never leave you child don't you know.
I am there while you grow .

I am there when you're good. I am there in the pain.
I am there when you're bad, and I love you just the same.

You can't change that fact.
I love you always to be exact!"

I'm an overcomer in this world below.
Because my Father in Heaven told me so.

He'd tell me not to hesitate.
And to not think I could wait,

to overcome, 'till I got to the pearly gate.
For then it will be a little too late.

For Jesus overcame while down here below.
And we should do the same that we must know.

We can call on his name, while we have now.
By an act of our will, now we can bow.

I'm an overcomer because I have my Daddy's blood in me.
The blood of Jesus that makes me free.

Through my veins it flows!
From my head right down to my toes.

It broke all the chains that really had me bound.
And now living here there is one thing I've found.

I don't need what this world offers, my Jesus will satisfy.
And that is why I'm living now to testify!

So I'm an Overcomer in this world below.
Because my Daddy in Heaven told me so.

He says, "My child Don't you fear.
For with you, I'm always near.

You can make it through the night.
You can make it through the fight.

You can make it through anything and I'll tell you why.
You'll be an Overcomer when on me you will rely.

Just on me, depend and cling.
And this song, Overcomer, you can sing!"

We have the Power! Do we not realize that? If we believe in Jesus Christ we have Power to Overcome any obstacle that is before us on this race. That is "if" we truly want to overcome. That is the question, "Do I really want to overcome? Do I really have to overcome? Can't I just go around this hurdle?" Well, yes you can go around that hurdle. But how bad do you want that prize? Do you want to be disqualified? I hope not. As Paul says in I Corinthians 9: 24-27 "Know ye not that they which run in a race run all, but one receiveth the prize? So run that ye may obtain. 25. And every man that competes for the mastery is temperate in all things. Now they do it to obtain a corruptible crown; but we an incorruptible. 26. I therefore so run, not as uncertainly; so fight I, not as one that beateth the air; 27. But I 'keep under my body (discipline), and bring it into subjection; lest that by any means, when I have preached to others, I myself should be a castaway (disqualified)." I don't know about you but I don't want to be disqualified. This scripture is not telling us to be competitive against other believers. Paul is referring to us taking a competitive attitude against the world, the flesh and the devil. James tells us in 1:12 "Blessed is the man that endureth temptation; for when he is tried he shall receive the crown of life, which the Lord hath promised to them that love him. 13. Let no man say when he is tempted, I am tempted of God; for God cannot be tempted with evil, neither tempteth he any man. 14. But every man is tempted, when he is drawn away of his own 'lust (desires) and enticed." See, our main obstacle we have to overcome first is "Us", "Self", "Flesh"! Which ever word you choose to use, "We" are the problem. It's not God! It's not Gods' problem in not overcoming.. It's not Gods' problem when we sin. And the devil isn't really the problem concerning us overcoming, either. Because Jesus our Savior already won the victory on the cross for us. Not that he does not tempt us, because he is going to do that, that is the devil. That is what he does. But it then lies within us, to choose. 1 Corinthians 15:56, 57 Paul says, "The sting of death is sin; and the strength of sin is the law. But thanks be to God, which giveth us the victory through our Lord Jesus Christ." We need to realize we already have the victory! As long as we trust in Jesus to save us and know that he has already fought our battles we will overcome. In Ephesians Paul talks about putting on the armor of God. In v. 16 he says, "Above all, taking the shield of faith, wherewith ye shall be able to quench all the fiery darts of the 'wicked (the devil)." Then Paul says in Colossians 2:15, "And having 'spoiled (disarmed) principalities and powers, he made a spectacle of them openly, triumphing over them in it." When we put our faith in Jesus Christ and what he has done for us on the cross we have the victory in every area of our lives! 1 John 4:4 says, "Ye are of God little children, and have overcome them (anti-christ spirit); because Greater is he that is in you, than he that is in the world." And John also says in 1 John 5:4, 5 "For whatsoever is born of God overcometh the world; and this is the victory that overcometh the world, even our faith. 5. Who is he that overcometh the world, but he that believeth that Jesus is the Son of God?" Oh! When we put our faith in Jesus we are victorious! He makes us victorious! When we die to our self and let Jesus reign on the throne of our hearts we are more than a conqueror through the blood of Jesus Christ! That is where the real battle lies. Believing that we are dead to sin and allowing Jesus to come alive and have complete control of our lives. It is all a matter of who or what we choose to yield to. Romans 6: 11 "Likewise 'reckon ye also yourselves to be dead indeed unto sin, but alive unto God through Jesus Christ our Lord. 12. Let not sin therefore reign in your mortal body, that ye should obey it in the lusts thereof. 13. Neither yield ye your members as instruments of unrighteousness unto sin; but yield yourselves unto God, as those that are alive from the dead and your members as instruments of righteousness unto God." Are we going to keep trying to go around that hurdle instead of over it. Are we going to just keep trying to ignore it, or overlooking it? You know there is no getting around it. We all have to deal with this issue of sin. It doesn't just go away or disappear on its on. No, we have to consciously choose are we going to keep it in our life and allow it to totally destroy us or not? You may not see it destroying you right now at the moment but look at the end of that road. And look right now at what you are missing out on if you choose not to overcome that sin in your life. See, Jesus wants us to overcome every obstacle in our way. And it is not for him that he wants us too. It is for us! So we will be blessed! Over and over in the book of Revelation, Jesus himself tells us what we can have if we overcome. Revelation 2:7, to eat of the tree of life. 2:11 He that overcometh shall not be hurt in the second death. 2:17, Jesus will give to eat of the hidden manna, and will give him a stone with a new name written in it. 2:26 Jesus promises he that overcometh and keepeth his works unto the end he will give power over the nations. And shall rule them with a rod of iron; as the vessels of a potter shall they be broken in pieces even as I received of my Father. And I will give him the morning star." In Revelation 3:5 Jesus promises he that overcomes shall be clothed in white raiment and Jesus will not blot out his name out of the book of life but will confess his name before the Father and his angels. Revelation 3: 21 "To him that overcometh will I grant to sit with me on the throne even as I also overcame I and am set down with my Father on his throne. 22. He that hath an ear let him hear what the Spirit saith unto the churches." And in Revelation 3:12 "Him that overcometh will I make a pillar in the temple of my God, and he shall go no more out; and I will write upon him the name of my God, and the name of the city of my God, which is new Jerusalem which cometh down out of Heaven from my God; and I will write upon him my new name."

"I Want to Be a Pillar"

I want to be a Pillar in the House of my God.
I want to stand strong and tall and with the Gospel be shod.

I want to overcome everything that comes my way.
I want to be a pillar strong and solid and in the storms never sway.

Oh! I want to be a Pillar useful to my Lord.
I want to be true and faithful, and stand on his Word.

Oh! I want to stand strong and always be there right from the start.
I want to be faithful doing my part!

A pillar is what I want to be.
Like a tall, strong oak tree.

For Jesus needs more pillars in his house today.
One that will hold it up when the storms come its way.

For a pillar will support it, so it'll never fall.
So I want to be a Pillar, nothing else that's all!

Jesus said in Revelation 3:12 "Him that overcometh will I make a pillar in the temple of my God and he shall go no more out: and I will write upon him the name of my God, and the name of the city of my God, which is new Jerusalem, which cometh down out of heaven from my God: and I will write upon him my new name." Jesus has a place for you one that is strong and true. He has a purpose for you. A very important part in his temple. For his kingdom. Jesus has awesome things ahead for those who choose to follow him. He loves us just the way we are, however, he has predestined us to be overcomers. He has a destiny and purpose for us. He wants to use us for his glory. However, he can't do it, not like he wants while we have sin in our life. He'll allow us to disqualify ourselves from our race if we choose not to overcome the sin in our life. He will just give our destiny to someone who will obey and yield to him. 2 Timothy 2: 20, 21 says, "But in a great house there are not only vessels of gold and of silver, but also of wood and of clay, and some to honor and some to dishonour. If a man therefore 'purge (cleanse) himself from these, he shall be a vessel unto honour, set apart and useful for the masters use, and prepared unto every good work." Oh! I don't know about you, but I want so bad for God to use me. And Gods' Word says right there if we purge ourselves from sin we will be fit for God to use us. He says we will be a vessel of honour. I don't know about you, but I want to be and do what God put me here for. I want so bad for Jesus to be lifted up in my life. I want so bad for others to see him in me!

"You Look Just Like Your Daddy!"

Has anyone ever told you lately,
you look just like your daddy?

You have his heart.You have his eyes.
And which really is no surprise.

For his blood runs right through every vein.
You can tell he's your Daddy, to see it's very plain.

You have his character shining out of you.
It shows in every single thing you do.

You have his heartbeat full of Love.
His Spirit you are so full of.

Full of mercy, truth and grace.
You have his Glory shining all over your face.

Your Daddy is gentle forgiving, kind and true.
Hey! He looks just like you!

I don't know about you I just want others to know that Jesus is real! And they will only know if we let him show. They say when a couple is married for a long time they start to look, talk and act like each other. That should happen with us and our Lord. I want to behold Gods' Glory more and more each step. So others will see only him and less of me. 2 Corinthians 3:17, 18 says, "Now the Lord is that Spirit. And where the Spirit of the Lord is there is Liberty. But we all with open face beholding as in a mirror the glory of the Lord are changed into the same image from glory to glory, even as by the Spirit of the Lord." Paul says as we behold the Lords glory it changes us. The more we spend time with our Lord, the more we look like him. Let me say the more we spend time with him and letting him speak to us out of his Word (our Bible) and we follow him then we start to look like him. We have to be very careful what are we beholding? What do we focus our thoughts, our minds, our hearts and our eyes and ears on throughout the day? Only when we give our lives to the Lord and yield completely to the Holy Spirit will we be blessed. It does make a difference what we behold. What we focus on most of the time will determine blessing or cursing. Joy or Sorrow. Life or Death. Too many people are living their lives far below what God has created them for. It is so sad! Too many people are seeing Psychiatrists for mental problems. Too many people are taking drugs because of fear, anxiety and depression. And it is so sad, because they do not have too. All they have to do is call on Jesus and give him everything. Give him all the pain and heartache. Give him all of your hopes and dreams. Instead of talking to some strange person about your problems, why not tell Jesus what you would tell that Psychiatrist. Jesus says in John 14:16 "And I will pray the Father, and he shall give you another 'Comforter (Helper), that he may abide with you for ever." In Acts 2:38, 39 Peter says, "Then Peter said unto them, Repent and be baptized everyone of you in the name of Jesus Christ for the forgiveness of sins, and ye shall receive the gift of the Holy Ghost. 39. For the promise is unto you and to all your children, and to all that are afar off, even as many as the Lord our God shall call. 40. And with many other words did he testify and exhort, saying, Save yourselves from this crooked generation."

You know the whole message and point of the Gospel is to give people Hope! The whole reason Jesus came was to give us Life! Jesus came to destroy the works of Satan. Too many are living far below than what God intended. We have to overcome. As Jesus says in Rev. 3:21 what we read earlier Just as he overcame and is sat down with the Father on his throne. Jesus promises us if we overcome Jesus will grant for us to sit with him on his throne. God has awesome plans for us. Let's not settle for less. For there is nothing at all greater than walking and talking with Jesus. Nothing at all greater than the Holy Spirit moving in you to experience new heights with him. Nothing greater when he calls you to come up higher!

"Come Up Higher!"

Oh! Hear the Spirit calling,
"Come Up Higher!"
Don't stay where you're at
in all the muck and all the mire.

Wake Up! Wake Up!
And open your eyes.
Stop making excuses
and lousy alibis.

God has such
awesome plans for you.
Get rid of all the sin
and Gods' plans pursue.

Take a look at where you're at and ask,
Do you really want to stay there?
There, hanging on to your sin
not getting anywhere?

Make up your mind and be determined.
You will no longer settle for less.
You will have what God wants.
And that is the best!

Make up your mind that you will
no longer let that sin have control.
You will heed the Spirits' Call
and surrender your soul.

You will surrender everything.
Your will and desire.
For you hear him calling,
for you to, "Come Up Higher!"

Like I said before, too many people are settling far below what God has for them. They are comfortable with and in their sin. God has put so much potential in us, and he expects us to use it. He has invested much in us. However, our desire for Him and his will has to be stronger than any desire to sin. Or we will stay on that same comfortable rung on the ladder and we will not get anywhere. We will not see what God has for us unless we repent of sin. And unless we have a strong desire for what he has for us. See, the thing is Jesus loves us always just the way we are. And he tells us that yes we can hang onto that sin and he'll still love us. But, he will get someone else to fulfill our destiny. To fulfill what he has called us to do. If we choose to stay where we are he will get someone else who will obey him and who moves on with him. God wants us to overcome the sin in our life and not allow anything to come in between our relationship with him. He wants us to be sensitive to his Spirit and obey him and let him have complete control every step of the way and he will lead us to greater heights.

"Greater Heights"

Those things that would to me be gain.
I now count but loss.
For Jesus took it all away
When I bowed at his cross.

For nothing I could do
could cleanse my soul within.
Jesus paid it all
Through Him I'm free from sin.

Greater Heights I must climb.
No looking back No wasting time.

For I have a goal to reach.
The everlasting Gospel to preach.

To Greater Heights he's moving me.
Though this Mountain only I see.
I'll leave all behind and follow him.
For Greater Heights he's moving me.

I've found a treasure in a field.
I'll sell all and buy. To God, my all I'll yield.

For Greater Heights he's moving me.
From my past he's set me free!

It is an awesome experience to serve our Lord Jesus. All he wants is to bless us. People are so deceived by Satan and by their own pride to think that they are happy and okay without Jesus. They have no idea what happiness, peace and joy is if they do not have Jesus. Apart from Jesus life is empty. There is no life apart from Him! I can't imagine living my life without Jesus. He is everything. We all need him whether we think we do or not. Because we all go through hard times. Even those who have been totally obedient have experienced times when we don't feel like his presence is with us. And we may suddenly feel like he has left us. We may get fretful, troubled and worried and wonder what did I do wrong. Lord, are you angry at me for something? Why am I feeling like this? During those times you have to remember and never forget that Jesus promised to never leave you and never forsake you! You are not Abandoned or left alone and forgotten! He has just gone on before you preparing the way. Keep seeking him and listening for him. And you'll soon hear him say,

"Come Up Hither!"

So many times Lord while following you,
along this straight and narrow path.
I'll be walking with you and then I won't feel you.
then I'll start to fear your wrath.

I'll start seeking your face once again.
And I'll wonder and I'll question you,
in what way did I sin?

Then I'll go a little bit farther
and I'll press on.
Then I once again will see your shining face.
Shining beautiful like the morning dawn.

Then you assure me everything's okay.
There are just new heights,
for you and I to climb.
And you call me
to Come up Hither!
For I am ready. Now it is time.
You tell me not to fear.
Everything will be just fine.

I don't always understand
where you are taking me.
And I don't always really need to know.
But if your face I seek to see
further on this journey your purposes will show!

And then one day soon, I'll hear you say
"Come up Hither"
for the last and final time.
When you'll call me
to my Home above.
Where there is peace sublime.

And I'll be with you, forever my Love.
Our Journey on earth will be done.
It shall be over, when once more
you Jesus Gods' Son,
say Come Up Hither!
Eternal life for you I have won!

All through our Journey with our Lord, those who walk with him, he goes before them. And prepares the way then says, "Come, follow me. or Come up Hither." Oh! I can't wait to hear him say, "Come Up Hither!" For the last and final time. I have such a longing to be with him in Heaven. This World has nothing to offer me.

"Lord, Come and Sweep Me Off of My Feet Again!"

Lord, when I reminisce about the time
You and I did meet.
One look at you was all it took.
To sweep me off of my feet.

You took my breath away.
And I didn't know what to say.
All I know is I am changed since that happy day.

And now I'm so longing to see you.
You are all that matters
No matter what I do.

You sweep me off of my feet.
Every time I think of you.
Oh! How I long to please you
in all I say and do!

Lord, I know this world is passing.
The way we know it, is coming to an end.
I can't wait, 'til you come back,
and sweep me off of my feet once again.

I know you'll sweep me off of my feet.
And take me high in the clouds,
when the next time we do meet.

So Lord please come back soon,
and sweep me off of my feet once again.
The way you did back then.

For I'm longing to see you.
You're the Love of my life!
Sweep me off of my feet,
out of this world of strife.

For I need you to rescue me,
out of this world of sin.
Oh! Lord please come and,
"Sweep Me Off Of My Feet Once Again!"

One day soon no one knows the day or the hour, Jesus will return. He is coming back for those who love him and are looking for him. Who love him enough to stay ready and are waiting for him. He is coming back to take us to an awesome place. A place called, "Heaven". Are you ready? If you're not. Get up and get ready! Call on Jesus, renounce Satan and repent of sin. And ask Jesus to fill you with his Holy Spirit and take control of your life. And Get into God's Word and obey it. And yield your members as members of righteousness now, instead of yielding to sin. God has such awesome plans for you. Plans for you before you were born. Plans of peace as Jeremiah says in 29:11, "For I know the thoughts that I think toward you, saith the Lord, thoughts of peace and not of evil, to give you 'an expected end (a future and a hope)."

As a Mother wakes her child up and tells them to hurry and get ready for school in hopes for a bright future. Hear Gods' Holy Spirit saying to us, be ready in hopes we will have what God has prepared for us in heaven. Peter says in 1:3, 4 "Blessed be the God and Father of our Lord Jesus Christ, which according to his abundant mercy hath begotten us again unto a 'lively (living) hope by the resurrection of Jesus Christ from the dead, 4. To an inheritance incorruptible, and undefiled, and that fadeth not away, reserved in Heaven for you," Jesus Christ has a place reserved in Heaven for you. As you believe in Jesus Christ as your Savior and Lord. And walk and talk with him and let him lead you. He will lead you to that place in Heaven he has reserved for you. Oh! How Awesome! Paul says in Romans 15:13, "Now the God of Hope fill you with all Joy and Peace in believing that ye may abound in Hope, through the power of the Holy Ghost."